Twilight Language
of the Nagual

Twilight Language
of the Nagual

The Spiritual Power of Shamanic Dreaming

MERILYN TUNNESHENDE

Bear & Company
Rochester, Vermont

Bear & Company
One Park Street
Rochester, Vermont 05767
www.InnerTraditions.com

Bear & Company is a division of Inner Traditions International

Library of Congress Cataloging-in-Publication Data
Tunneshende, Merilyn.
  Twilight language of the Nagual : the spiritual power of shamanic dream-
ing / Merilyn Tunneshende.— 1st ed.
     p. cm.
  ISBN 1-59143-041-0
  1. Tunneshende, Merilyn. 2. Juan, Don, 1891- 3. Shamans—Mexico—
Biography. 4.   Dreams—Miscellanea. 5.   Shamanism—Mexico—
Miscellanea. I. Title.

  BF1598.T86A3 2004
  299'.93—dc22
                                        2004010300

Printed and bound in Canada by Webcom

10 9 8 7 6 5 4 3 2 1

Text design and layout by Rachel Goldenberg
Feather illustration by Mary Anne Hurhula

This book was typeset in Sabon with AlParmaPetit as the display typeface

To the wisdom of the child within us all,
to the exquisite poetry of silence,
to our natural luminous awareness,
and to joy and freedom.

Contents

Part Two — WISDOM AND APPLICATION

Acknowledgments

I wish to express my gratitude to all the beings of the lower realms who have taught me about suffering, longing, and regret; to those beings of the realms of Earth who have taught me to understand the trade-offs of temporal existence, and of the solace in the tenderness of true human affection; and to the beings of the Celestial realms who have taught me of the time-less, of evolution, of the refinements of subtle mind, of joy, and of the love and liberation beyond death.

Two roads diverged in a wood, and I . . .
I took the one less traveled by,
And that has made all the difference.

ROBERT FROST

Prologue

First Glimpses
of the Code

Over my lifetime I have made a careful scientific study of the religious, the ecstatic, the transcendental, and the enlightened experience. This study began as a child and it has continued throughout my entire life, well beyond graduate school and on into the experiential teachings of shamans and mystics. I have been blessed with what my mother called "true language abilities," which she defined as a peculiar manner of understanding, seeing, and communicating with energy directly without the limitations of a particular cognitive system. I perceive, speak with, and listen directly to the essences of many different types of being. These abilities often manifest themselves in waking visions, in seeing beyond, and in awakened Dreaming, in which wisdom is communicated via its direct language—a transmission of movement from within inner silence and received as an experiential understanding that I can then interpret, and that I may later confirm to be truth and share with others for their benefit.

As an adult, I searched out this phenomena in the accounts of the lives of religious saints, mystics, and the prophets; from healers, yogis, masters, and realized beings to the esoteric mystery traditions; in ancestral gods and spirits; within psychology and psychiatry; in archetypes, hermeneutics, cryptography, anthropology, and the science of physics; and via the study of dreams and trance. I sought out shamans, lamas, priests and priestesses, and medicine men and women for good counsel, so as to receive their blessings upon these abilities. The Tibetans understand it and describe the energy as a sacred marriage of profound wisdom to skillful means, which is like an elixir that is poured into a vessel, a body. The language is one they poetically refer to as the "Twilight Language." This language comes from the enlightened realms. Certain individuals can understand or interpret it for the purpose of recovering and perhaps revealing, if the time is right, ancient and evolutionary treasures and teachings that lead others toward enlightenment, healing, empowerment, and liberation.

The shamans of the Yuman native culture understand it also, perhaps best of all, and they call this ability Dream Power. One who possesses this sought-after gift is titled a Kwaxot. Yuman natives do not have a religion. Rather, they base their entire body of shamanic wisdom and medicine, and the selection of their leaders, upon Dream Power. These initiated individuals have the ability to understand this Twilight Language or the language of Dream Power so profoundly that they can interpret any dream accurately and speak with convincing, empowered wisdom and eloquence when they serve as leaders. They also have the ability to make their Dreams manifest in the waking world of the collective, to see into energy directly, and to enter into the dreams of others for sacred medicine purposes.

It has been my great fortune to be led to magnificent individuals of many different global traditions and cultures—from temple mystics to hunter-gatherers—who have cultivated, cherished, understood, and empowered this ability. They have all given me their blessing. It is the Twilight Language itself that has led me to those who can communicate with it directly. As a result of their seasoned development and Dream Power guidance, I have grown to understand the treasure and I continue to grow in this understanding.

What I put forth here are gems from the treasure chest for collective joy, evolution, and liberation. I offer them up freely for the fulfillment of every desire and as medicine. These wisdom gems are not all that has been revealed within the chest, but they are truly valuable, and it is permissible to share facets of them. I have found in experimenting, and in sharing with doctors, psychiatrists, psychologists, scientists, documenters, spiritual seekers, artists, and everyday people worldwide, that these jewels bring profound, blessed change for the better. This is simply excellence, and it brings us answers to many benevolent prayers and a gradual severing of the ties that bind us to delusion, to misery, to slavery, and to division.

So how shall you benefit from this book?

The body of this book consists of three main aspects. One aspect is that of initiatory experiences that will assist the readers in understanding and experiencing the profound nature of the wisdom itself. The second aspect is that of carefully selected practices that are included for the readers at the end of each chapter. These practices are designed to be suitable and beneficial for any level, from novice to professional, from layperson, to adept, to practitioner. Their purpose is to give experiential tasks that may be successfully applied in one's own life and work. The third aspect is that of practical wisdom and applications, and it is suitable for everyone seeking examples, cases, and studies of putting this work into practice directly in the worlds we live in.

The entire book is written as a seamless marriage of art and cathartic recounting, psychology, alternative healing, shamanism and spirituality, religious experience and objective science, and practical guidance. It is written in this manner because I reside and practice in all of these worlds and because the divisiveness in our existential realities is one cause of the maladies. The experiences and wisdom are genuine and the explanations are lucid and clear. The scope moves from the interlacing of subjectivities to the sublime witnessing of the miraculous in the purely objective mode.

This work can stand alone or be combined with other disciplines. It is artful, powerful, and effective; yet that is all focused into the strong essence of humility and love, and applied in a compassionate, honest, and selfless manner. The work, the recounting, the energy, and the practices transcend the barriers of the written word, of cognition, culture, politics, religion, and dogma. Anyone with any educational background or belief system, from any walk of life, can approach this and benefit in some manner. The practices can be applied and experienced, the stories and accounts may be learned from, appreciated, and enjoyed, and the energy may be transmitted directly. Thus at whatever level you may find yourself, there is some aspect of this work that will apply and be beneficial.

Everything offered here has been thoroughly tested by myself and my colleagues in collaboration with medical doctors, psychologists, and psychiatrists. It is all totally sound and credible, highly benevolent and successful, applicable and approachable, mature and sane—and yet enjoyable, spontaneous, and fun, all at the same time. Even though it reaches and thinks far outside the box, and discovery and surprise await, the reader and practitioner and professional may feel totally confident that this is benevolently intended, for the greatest benefit, for it is thinking and living only inside the box that has created all of our problems.

I highly encourage the reader to release the self and suspend judgment. Go on the journey and then investigate. Allow the energy and the momentous mass of effort behind this work to evolve consciousness, to educate, and to provide all the guidance and corroboration you will require to proceed further, carrying it on into your own field of endeavors.

I humbly offer the experiential aspects and the practical applications of this work for the benefit of all sentient beings.

Thank you, and enjoy.

Take all of your expertise and trade it for wonder.
SIDDHARTHA GAUTAMA BUDDHA

Introduction

In the Beginning

It is very difficult for children, fresh perceivers who can see purely, to correct or disagree with the misperceptions of love, dreams, God, the Creation, and death that are spoon-fed to them by all those around them, supposed authoritarian experts who seemingly "know," and yet never communicate with God or claim to understand creation themselves. These knowledge-able beings appear to be victims of self-inflicted excommunication and long-repressed hallucinations. It is obvious to the seeing child, for example, that God is not exclusively masculine, but just try to interject this, in a childlike way, into daily "rational Western" conversation.

When I was a child, surrounded by questionable, controlling "scholars" and laypersons of God in the machine, I had a dream of the Creation, the Tree of Life, and what really happened in Genesis. I was then being raised on the mystical biblical stories of the Torah, the five books of Moses, and before I knew it, my dreams started exploring the tale of creation. This was, for some reason, a source of concern for my parents.

It all began the summer my father was completing his master's degree in celestial mechanics at Yale University. We were renting a home on Charter Oak Street in New Haven, Connecticut, at that time, from an old woman who lived in the basement apartment, a woman I was never allowed to see or visit, but who was reported to be there by both my mother and my father in "presence."

She never came up, and as a mere toddler I was never permitted to go down to the underworld where she lived. I never even heard her voice or saw her shadow; but at times, especially at night, I could sense an old female whispering and wafting up through the floorboards, creaking and groaning like dry wood with a heavy weight on it. In my dreams, I could see the black void that was down there and inside the void was the presence of living light, and the all-encompassing awareness of that old woman. This abstract woman and her power of presence, this grand dame of all, later became a Twilight Language teacher to me. She is named doña Celestina.

When my father received his degree, we moved to Maryland, where my parents purchased a townhouse with a large basement that became my private playroom. In fact, just like the old woman I almost lived in this basement, until I began elementary school. I played in a solitary way and whispered down there all day, except when my favorite television show, *Pete the Pirate*, aired each afternoon. I listened to this show about a pirate and a captive mermaid even when our television screen was on the blink and went black. I only came up for this and to eat my meals, to bathe and prepare for bed, sleep, and dreams.

I didn't realize it then, but I was a being in Dreaming within the womb space of that old woman, the one who could not be seen, but about whose presence one had best be assured. She was in-dwelling spirit, lest one take a false step. One must be careful around the spirits. Her presence always communicated with signs at first and then whispers, and she didn't concur with the content of my punishing-masculine-God bedtime stories. She thought my father a poor storyteller and told me so, repeatedly.

She did, however, enjoy my mother's take on the Creation

and advised me once to observe in a dream how my mother ascended and descended the central flaming stairway within our home, carrying a huge knife that she kept secluded under the sink. This was her edge of protection, I was told, a knife that had been given to her, to women, by that dark old-woman presence, a knife she used for prowling and stalking anything that did not belong in our house, just like a lioness baring claws on the hunt. What she caught would be carved up and if it could not account for itself then, it would be fed to the pride. That old woman presence showed me some of the "woman's sacred fire"—lightning halos around my mother's head that could be seen when I was fully awake and the yellow fire circling around the pupils of her eyes when she stared in my direction.

Naturally when I went down the stairs daily to play in the basement, I would chatter to the old woman's womb about the meaning of such visions. I had never yet heard a word that could describe my experiences accurately, and so I called them "it." Thus, I saw "it." I dreamed "it." I spoke with "it," listened to "it," and loved "it." Several of the women in our maternal line also seemed to sense "it," for they caught on, and took to protecting their own throats from whispers, wrapping them up with scarves when they were in my company.

At about this time, my mother's throat swelled to the size of a melon and afterward, mine did too. After the swelling went down, respected and beloved elder members on both sides of my family came out of the woodwork to visit me, and they talked with me frequently to test my verbal capacity. They asked me to learn the meaning and pronunciation of words like *ventriloquist*, and they applauded my ability to state verbatim anything that I had been told, as though I had always known it.

The elders' pronouncement was that I had "it." My mother privately explained to me that "it" ran on both sides of the family and that if one had "it," one needed nothing else—and that if one didn't have "it," well, nothing else one had was of any consequence. I contented myself with this, and I began to nurture "it" with my every thought, word, and action.

After this incident, the old woman installed a spirit guardian for me down there in the basement, one who would watch my play, teach me about "it," and protect and love me. My time in the basement began to agree more and more with my dreams and I could actually distinguish the outline and the inner voice of this presence, a stately old native spirit that I first called Grandfather. He told me that there were many such presences in our lineage, much spirit, and that some of them were utterly untraceable to the ordinary world.

Grandfather loomed like a pillar of cloud and knew everything there was to be known. Between the two of them—Grandfather, who met me in many forms, one as the being I now call don Juan; and the old woman's womb, who met me as the mentor I call doña Celestina—they corrected my view of creation. They recounted events that altered my perception of all consensus agreements and of communication, telling me new stories, giving me dreams, and asking that I pay special attention to the powers and gifts I was inheriting from my familial lineages and from their lineages.

Both mentors told me that "it" was something completely new, and that as a result, I must listen very carefully to everything they were going to share with me, listen with love. They expressed to me that no one living really understands love. They saw this as a problem, a challenge, and so I would have to learn. I saw through their counsel that people have truly lost or never found the love inside of them and that this is a dark scourge that could destroy everything. I plainly perceived how humans often repress and control their own experiences, of death for example, and how many sense next to nothing of how they have come to be here.

I realized that human beings can frequently focus all of their understanding or misunderstanding on the meaning of words, in order to buffer themselves from their own experiences. They also worship the phantom in the window, their idol on the screen or in the smoking mirror, which is often nothing more than their own poor reflection. I was able to discern that since their experiences and their meaningful but limited words and images cannot ever fully agree, this leaves huge gaps in them. It makes them confused, unwise, forgetful, small-minded, sad, and hungry, and sometimes, it eventually even makes them into liars.

I saw clearly how humans will often only focus their attention on what they are told or wish to be told that they can consume, know, and possess, and on what they later tell themselves about their experiences. This puts them at odds. They even differ as to their interpretations and so they seldom ever really agree with one another. They cannot rely on their direct experiences and genuine memories for wisdom to clear up the matter, because in truth they have had none.

To learn the language of medicine for this, my mentors expressed, I would experience their presence as something not unlike true human beings. I would be empty. When I was ready, I would then see it all through their eyes, hear it with their ears to assist my own, and that would be the real beginning, a rebirth of everything for me. I would descend and ascend a flaming and watery stairway of rainbow awareness, traveling its fathoms and its lengths with prowess and understanding. I was cautioned that I should not let anything shield me from receiving this proper inspiration of seeing and hearing, and that I should never fear "it." Instead, I should be wary of what I would be like, what life and death would be like, were I to live without "it."

They then became still for a time and let their language grow inside me like a hardy survivor, an impossible jimsonweed creeping out of a stranglehold crack in the cement of an old, dark basement. What follows are my recountings and experiential tales gleaned from my interactions with them—teachings and wisdom gems written in the Twilight Language.

Part One
The Initiations

1

The Butterfly Crowned Serpent

After childhood, spirits and presences kept silent, mostly, until the death of my fiancé while I was in college. I had realized by then, both academically and instinctively, that just as "God" and "life" are not as they have been portrayed by our teachers of perception, neither is "death" at all like its descriptive glosses. However, I hadn't yet seen the possibilities. Frankly, the world seemed lost, stuck, and blind. In suffering and desperation, I undertook a journey of seeing, awakening, and discovering in my departed beloved's honor, and it was during this sojourn that I first interacted as an adult with the living physical presences of don Juan and doña Celestina de la Soledad, just as I had spiritually foreseen that I would while playing as a child in the basement.

Don Juan was apparently, at that time, living in the desert of the Yuma Indians, and doña Celestina was seemingly living a little farther south among the Cocopah people. I had stopped in Yuma, Arizona, to make some inquiries about travel yet farther south into Mexico, and don Juan simply appeared as though he had been awaiting my arrival. He actually met my train near where it rolled in and then proceeded to imperiously guide me in that solitary place. Upon seeing him, something in me just stopped and there was no doubt in my being. He spent our first months familiarizing me with some of his favorite local haunts and completely redirected my journey.

He had a strange way about him, but I was alone and friendless after the tragedy and not given to complaints about such trivial things. According to him, he could "See"—a manner of perceiving energy directly—that I had recently experienced the death of a loved one and that I was thus in touch with the spirits. That and the sheer unique magnificence of his presence are what stopped me. He also wielded the peculiar skill of Dream Power, and in fact he was a consummate artist of dreams, their interpretations, and the energies they offer us. He endeavored to instruct me in the value of Dream Power and to imbue me with it, as a vehicle for personal transformation, energetic and spiritual communication with those human and beyond human, and the eventual liberation of being, or transcendence. He indicated that I was marked for this instruction and empowerment because of my recent and profound brush with death and due to my capacity for deep, yet awakened trance and Dreaming.

Don Juan saw Dreaming to be a level of awareness through which we access the experience of the world beyond the barriers of our limited words, consensus, and cognition—a way to access the world of the direct experience of energy, being, and the powers of intent. Words, as he saw it, can often define, buffer, and imprison us in the shabby hovel of what we like to call the ordinary consensus agreement. They function as perceptual glosses divorced from the energy that is not included within their definitions, and from the power that energy lends to our acts. This energy is our profound right and inheritance as sentient beings. Dreaming practices are then one vehicle for making contact with that energy and for liberating ourselves into our rightful inheritance.

Seeing, as don Juan explained it to me, is a skill that we can use when we are awake in ordinary, everyday reality to access our genuine perceptions of direct experiences with energy, freed, as we are in Dreaming, from the perceptive glosses attached to words, to a priori and to past experience. Seeing is in the now. It is not knowing, but understanding. It is being able to choose based on this new dynamic. Thus, as he stated it, he could actually See my condition without the need for me to offer any explanations to him, and he could therefore take the proper actions accordingly, via energy that transcends the boundaries of limited consensus.

Over time, the actions he took also facilitated my acquaintance with doña Celestina, and that was how the whole thing began. Doña Celestina worked with Dream Power as well; her emphases were "energetic intervention" and "conflict resolution," as she called them. In other words, the locals thought she was a powerful witch or a wise woman, but she was even more, almost a form of justice. So, as I had sensed they would as a child, my mentors met me in person in a desert below sea level, and they began to whittle away at all my views of creation, of life, of death, of language, and of love.

They replaced my emptied, cleansed perceptions with new instruction. Some of their lessons came in the form of specific practices that they admonished me to undertake. Others came in the form of ancient and future teachings presented in the now, and specially created stories, and yet others were totally experiential, witnessed with my naked awareness and my naked heart, for these according to my mentors were essential prerequisites of true Seeing and thus of the true understanding that leads to wisdom.

The first specially designed teaching story or parable of Twilight Language that don Juan shared with me after that initial meeting was relevant to me and to all beings precisely because it was about nonnegotiable death and about the choices that our spirits must make after death. It has remained one of the most valuable bits of wisdom that has ever been shared with me, in addition to being one of the most tender tales I have ever been told.

Shortly after my arrival in Arizona, following a long walk, we were seated on the ground outside the confines of the reservation with our backs leaning against pillar stones. We watched the desert sunset ablaze, its colors shining upon Avik'wal, the sacred hill in the Yuman desert of the dead where departing spirits must remain, completing their unfinished business. As the sun descended, he began to speak.

"There were three individuals who all died in the same tragic road accident," don Juan said as he looked into my eyes and his reflected the sunset. "One was an extremely wealthy middle-aged man. One was a working man of average means. And one was a six-year-old boy. After a time in spirit transition, each one found themselves at a gateway, a crossroads, a tunnel. Within the tunnel was a guardian and this guardian spoke its challenge to the three newly dead.

"'You have each died. You will not go back again to live. Yet you must each go back and select one thing from your lives to present as the representative, the token of the lives that you have lived,' the guardian said. 'This will determine where you go from here. To accomplish this task, you will be given what would be the equivalent of one day in the world from which you have come. No one from your life there will be able to see or hear you during this special time, so do not waste any of it on that. Select your gift and then return here to where you now wait. Do not become lost in forgetfulness or remorse.'

"With that, all three of them found themselves with the ability to move back into the domain of their everyday lives as though they were within a lucid dream. The first gentleman went straight to his mansion. He surveyed, with the relish of one last look, all of the fine collectible items he had amassed during the course of his life—his antiques, crystal, finely crafted porcelain, massive furnishings, exquisite luxuries, and world-famous art. From all of this he had one treasure he loved most of all: a priceless solid-gold Roman Imperial candelabra from the time of Jesus, his favorite period of history. He retrieved this from his household and went back to wait at the entrance to the tunnel.

"The second man had no fine things and he was very embarrassed about the stage of life in which his death had caught him. He had not found the best in himself. He was not happy. Neither was he successful. His home was a cheap, filthy dump. None of his personal relationships had worked out for him. He had never allowed himself to fully reveal, accept, express, or experience pure genuine love. He had made many mistakes and none of them were completely corrected. His human values had been, well, less than admirable for the most part. He had dealt somewhat dishonestly with his fellows and was a liar, a misrepresenter, and a braggart without cause, mostly about trivial, petty things. In the light of the end of his life, he saw all of this with painful clarity.

"He retrieved an empty journal from his abode and began the task of writing a long lament and a recapitulation, a recounting and an expression of remorse for every lousy, substandard, cowardly, selfish moment he had ever lived or failed to live. It was this journal that he intended as his offering to the throne of heaven, in the hopes that in some small way it could atone for the sins he had committed and for all the good that he had failed to do.

"The last of the three was the young boy, who had no fine things and no long life filled with mistakes to apologize for. All the boy possessed that was worth anything to him, all he truly loved, was a dead butterfly collection. Each of the specimens had been found on the ground in perfect condition after having died. He hadn't killed a single one. He had merely retrieved each from its fate with infinite care. He went into his childhood bedroom and selected from the glass case the most sublimely beautiful specimen he had ever found.

"Thus at the end of the day allowed them, the three recently departed spirits returned to the tunnel and to the passageway to the light, there to wait before the entrance to the throne of heaven. At the appointed time, the guardian angel returned to demand that each one bring forth his gift in turn. The first man approached and proudly set down a twenty-four-karat-gold Roman candelabra. He placed it before the threshold of the throne of heaven. And it was judged as a gift and nothing more.

"The second man approached and laid down his apologetic before the angel.

"This was judged as an attempt. There was silence. Now it was the boy's turn to approach and he trembled with fear at the pitiful gift he held in his hand. He was not the rich master of a large estate, nor had he lived a long life that could be counted as an epic tale of his vast experiences. Still, he was no coward. He had what he had to offer and that was all. He was sincere. Trembling, he approached the light and gently placed his dead butterfly at the angel's feet.

"Suddenly a celestial chorus rained down upon the boy like a waterfall and the finger of God emerged from the light to touch the immobile wings of the butterfly. The vaulted heavens opened. Instantly the butterfly flew up in the most exquisite pattern and with its flight the boy was lifted up through the golden white celestial light to a place that the others could only imagine.

"When the light receded from above and only the light at the end of the tunnel remained, the two men were taken off to the side, away from the tunnel and the light, to a darker place of instruction. For though they had witnessed everything that transpired, they did not understand why the boy's gift had been selected and theirs had not."

I was shivering uncontrollably when don Juan finished

recounting his tale, even though it was a warm desert twilight. The owls were out. I felt as though I had been bathed in ice water. My lower lip was trembling and my eyes were so watery that the entire landscape looked like an impressionistic painting done in periwinkle blue.

"The journey is not for cowards," don Juan said as he turned again to me. "You are not at all fearful, but you are tender hearted and appalled by the condition of life on Earth. You think that this is well hidden, but it isn't. It's obvious. Now you have seen how beings can die here and this is even more horrifying for you, but it doesn't have to be that way, or rather, beings do not have to die in a squalid manner. You can't speak now. You don't know how to tell me what is in your heart, what has happened, but it's not necessary. I can see through all that."

"Someone I love died horribly with unfinished business," I blurted out.

"And you think this is somehow your fault?" he asked me with a sardonic inflection.

"No, it isn't. He offered himself. But I am beginning to realize that how we live and how we die affects everything. It affects all life and awareness wherever we are. It affects our journeys afterward."

"So it is," don Juan mused.

"What can we do about it?" I asked him.

"Change the way you live and the way you die," he challenged.

"In your tale, the individuals had no time!" I insisted.

"Exactly, we have no time," he affirmed.

"The boy, he used something else, something other than his intellect, something other than his memories, other than time," I baited.

"He used his heart, but first we have to have one," don Juan conceded.

"That's the problem, isn't it? The world has no heart. The boy didn't need time! All he had was a handful of dead moments and still he made the right choice. He chose sincerely with love and humility. That was his wisdom and it was more moving in the eyes of heaven than all earthly riches or mental exercises."

"So much for your lost tongue," don Juan smiled slyly. "You are right," he smirked. "The whole civilized world goes around wearing watches and complaining that they have no time. They also say that time is money, so they must not have any of that either. Time is money, so make the most of every cent."

I began to laugh. This old fellow was quite profound, unconventional, and humorous. It was strange, but I also found him very handsome. Don Juan raised his brow as if he had read my thoughts.

"What causes beings to lose heart, so that they make all the wrong choices?" I asked.

"Oh, myriad things," he sighed. "Fear, envy, denial, anger, vanity, abuse, self-pity, self-importance, greed, want, gluttony, ignorance, hunger for knowledge . . . or perhaps they were just made to be stupid. They certainly don't teach love to one another. It has to grow up like a wild weed. And when they find it, if ever, they are so afraid of it that they try to convert it into what they are or even kill it. They replace it with the mirror reflection of themselves and then say 'There . . . there now.' They want carbon copies of themselves, false agreement in every petty way, and then they complain when that doesn't satisfy."

"I know a story about that!" I exclaimed.

"Let's hear it," don Juan said. "C'mon, hit me with it. Give me your best shot straight to the heart."

"There was once a king who lived alone in his palace surrounded by his court," I began. "His only relief was the nightly song of a bird in the tree outside his bedroom window. Each and every night the bird would come to perch on a different branch of the tree and sing a beautiful song, never the same way twice.

"The court found out about the nightly serenades and became jealous of the king's attentions and affections. To vainly reacquire them, they constructed a solid-gold music box in the form of a bird and presented it to the king as a gift one night while in his bedchamber. He could listen to the mechanical bird any time he wished and keep it with him in his room, or he could even carry it around in his pocket.

"At first the king was enchanted and didn't notice that the song was always the same. He listened to the music box over and over, so often that he forgot to listen for his beloved in the tree outside his bedroom window. Eventually the little bird stopped coming to sing for him and went to sing alone in the tree of a far-off field.

"After a time, the king grew heartsick with the monotonous song of the music box. He went to his window to listen for the bird, but she was gone. So he continued to listen to his toy bird and then one day the toy broke. The king became very ill and the court was selfishly fearful of his demise. They also felt some remorse for what they had done.

"They sent out an emissary to look for the wild bird and they found her, singing alone in a tree by the river. They tried to bribe her with food to get her to follow them back, but she wasn't interested in their morsels. Then they confessed to her that the king was sick.

"Without another thought she flew back to him and began to sing in the tree outside his window. Her song had grown even more beautiful through her sadness and isolation, so lovely in fact that the king roused himself from his sickbed to ask her where she had been and why she had left him.

"She replied that she had been hurt by his actions and by his lack of loyalty. Each night she had come freely of her own volition to offer her songs for him. There was never any question or doubt of her love for him nor any need of ownership. It did not even matter that he had become fascinated by a mechanical song, but what did matter very much was that he abandoned the window and had stopped listening to the genuine, which was the only thing he had ever truly loved in his life.

"The king, heart struck, asked her why she had come back then. She replied, 'Because I love you and they told me you have realized your true heart.' It was hard for him to say that he had, for he was very saddened by the choice he had made. The little bird saw his sadness and stayed to sing in the tree for him all night."

"But he still died, didn't he?" don Juan inferred.

"Yes, he died that night, listening to the song," I answered.

"Was the little bird responsible then for his death?" he asked.

"No," I answered. "She brought him medicine so that he could have a good life and a good death."

"Did the little bird deserve to be imprisoned by the court in order to keep him alive?"

"No," I replied, "and he would never have allowed that, not after what he had learned."

"Neither are you responsible for the death in the world, nor for the manner of it, and you do not need to be imprisoned to keep it alive," don Juan consoled. His left eye was slightly moist. "Just bring them your medicine. That's all you can do." And with those words and feelings, he concluded our storytelling for the night and we walked to his home in silence.

When we arrived at his house, don Juan lit a kerosene lantern.

"How do I find the medicine I am to bring?" I asked him as he unrolled a straw mat and laid it out on the earthen floor.

"Oh, you already have it," he affirmed. "You just need to refine it and concentrate it for potency. Medicine people spend a long and solitary time allowing their power to come to them. I did the same thing myself, so we are alike in that. You see, power asks that we release certain human attachments, so that we have a privacy and a sacred empty space for power or spirit to come and fill."

"And then what?" I queried.

"Well, that depends on the power or spirit that comes," don Juan said with a grin. He was goading me. "Don't try to imagine it," he continued in a more soothing tone. "Just remain empty and detached, as you are now. The power will often come to you in Dreaming first, and then it will follow you into your world of everyday life, asking, even insisting that you dismantle the artificially contrived structure in order to make room for it."

He rolled out another straw mat for me beside his own and motioned for me to lie down on it. Then he blew out the kerosene lantern. I lay still there in the dark. Ever since I was a child, and especially again now, since my life had changed so suddenly and radically, once the lights were out and I was in bed, I would feel and see an energy descending on me like a sparkling, clarified, purplish golden and green-black vapor. When that energy would come, I'd know that it meant I was in for strong dreams.

It felt as though don Juan and I were lying with our mats upon an ancient barge as it floated down a deep, silent river into the sea. My entire life dissolved before me as though we were cruising on the river of the dead, and the dark sea of that awareness. I felt no delusion, no attachments, no concern about my whereabouts or my nonordinary circumstances. I had no fear, no doubt, and no guilt. Wonder was pleasant but I did not have any need to question. I was deconfigured. I understood that I had made the right decision, the only decision in fact for me. I was one with the presence of the only energy that could satisfy my being, or make existence real. I was following my heart.

That was the way the dream began. It began with love and freedom. The enlightening sun rose and there was nothing but golden white light and a singing tone. Vibrant ecstasy permeated everything, but it did not at all disturb the calm and the peace. Liberation and sacred union fully merged in the same timeless eternity, as an energetic conjoining, a marriage wine, but not in the conventional sort. It dripped from the cosmos like dew onto all life and awareness. I fully understood the beloved and that we were marrying, but it was impossible to put the rapture into anything resembling words. There was no saying of "I do." It was more like "I love," or "we love and that's our freedom forever."

When I awoke into what don Juan liked to call the waking awareness of everyday life, I realized that there was compassionate action implied by what I had experienced. A gesture was required, a profound overt act. I was going to empty out my life and make room for all this. I would need to do whatever the energy might ask of me during my life, for this—this ability to Dream and the medicine don Juan would teach me—this was my beloved, my luminous evolutionary body, my own heart speaking, my twin being, my energetic counterpart.

At that moment there was a knock at the door. I arose from the straw mat and opened the door into the morning light. There stood a young American woman, a social worker I had seen in town. She was holding two new, warm, patterned blankets for don Juan's house as a present, a gesture of goodwill. She was also a recent visitor and new resident of this town and was trying to meet all the locals in and around the reservation area.

I introduced myself to her and she returned the courtesy. She was about my age, perhaps just a little older. She was simply, mildly pretty and I almost liked her, yet don Juan had advised me not to become involved with the begging social services. So just like an Indian, I distanced myself from her and the trappings of her world ever so slightly. I told her I had just risen and that don Juan was not about at the moment, which was the truth, for he had gone out walking early in the morning. I asked her to leave the blankets outside the doorway and said that I would inform don Juan regarding who had brought them.

She then asked if I would be staying with him. I replied, "Of course." She seemed truly touched and moved by this and smiled at me for the first time. Before departing, she asked me to accept one of the blankets for myself. I regarded her carefully and told her that I could not account for what don Juan might do with them, if anything at all, that he had already given me any bedding I needed, but that they would no doubt be put to use somewhere on the reservation.

After the woman left I began to look around the house for something to prepare for our breakfast. All I could find was a gourd filled with blue cornmeal and another filled with raw honey. I went to the outdoor spigot, freshened up, and filled a fired clay pot with water to start it boiling. I decided to cook outside at the fire pit, even though there was a double burner inside, because there was wood for a fire and it was a beautiful, cheerful morning in the desert.

I rolled up our straw mats, placed them against one wall, and opened up the front and back doors and wooden-slat windows to let fresh air and light into the small house. I was humming and stirring the bubbling corn cereal when don Juan appeared on the horizon, wearing a straw hat. As soon as he got a bit closer, I waved to him. Once he had ambled down the sandy path and seated himself on a log by the cooking fire and I had poured us bowls of hot corn mush and mugs of tea, I told him about the blankets.

He waved them off and looked up at me from his steaming cereal, soberly at first and then smiling broadly. That was the only gesture he made to let me understand how he felt about it. "So you're with me then?" he affirmed. "You're the one I'm looking for, the one I'm interested in. Learn and be here."

"Yes," I said.

"You don't want to change your mind?" he asked calmly.

"No," I said.

"Good," he replied, "because I have much I'd like to share with you."

Practice One

Dreaming a Good Life

1. Enter into the state of Dreaming with the intent to be aware and awakened within it. To begin, as you drift into trance-like sleep, focus on the transitions from wakefulness into relaxation and then from relaxation into a peaceful, enhanced, more heightened awareness.

2. Enjoy each transition. Allow your body to become deeply satisfied at each level. Once you enter into the visionary heightened awareness of pre-Dreaming, before Dreaming and sleep, focus your intent upon imageless, formless, light-filled, ecstatic love from the heart, freedom and peace. See this burning from within.

3. Enter directly into the transition of Dreaming and sleep without losing this continuity, without losing this imageless, golden-light-filled, awakened state of being.

4. Realize this awakened awareness in Dreaming is our original, natural luminosity. Allow Dreaming to fully become this clarified state of natural luminosity and listen to its sound, a simple tone that is the beginning wisdom of the Twilight Language.

5. Do not digress from this state into those of generated imagery. Remain here. Realize that this is the place to go for enlightenment, for comfort and solace, for guidance and peace, and the level of awareness to reach at the moments before and during death. This is also the place to go during good meditation. This is your natural, delusion-free being.

6. Practice this Dreaming task repeatedly throughout your entire life. If you are able to enter into this awareness during meditation, relaxation, Dreaming, and during the actual death process, you will not become lost in delusion or suffering. You will find your refuge in life. And you will go directly out of all entanglements easily, with awakened and sublime awareness through the crown of the head. Doing so at death, you'll not be subjected to an undesirable return or unwanted forms of being.

2

Little Blood Moon

We took those blankets to a giveaway ceremony. Don Juan shared his own resources with me and he also asked that I share my inner resources, my very being, with him. To begin the timeless link with me from childhood and girlhood to womanhood in a tangible way, don Juan and I had frequent animated conversations about my being raised as a little child in the basement playroom. He found the whole visionary, spiritual experience to be a fascinating tale of multiple levels of reality, all perceived simultaneously. The tale, he said, was filled beyond the brim with active manifestations of genuine and authentically perceivable energetic entities and spirits. With the intent of enriching my awareness of the entire experience, he provided me with lengthy and practical energetic insights, often mixed with the ancient wisdom of a Mesoamerican creation story.

He had learned of this particular creation story from a Mayan friend, a peerless healer and Dreamer. Don Juan felt that the story paralleled my experiences to such a high degree that recounting it would be a useful teaching tool. Merely recounting, however, was never in the cards for don Juan. He carefully, artfully wove my own experiences into the story, while taking me entirely out of the picture so as to focus the tale on the most universal axis, something that everyone feels, the pain of being alone and having to overcome hells, suffering, and death.

"There was once a young maiden by the name of Little Blood Moon," don Juan began, "which also means 'early menstruation' or 'red lunar eclipse.' She was not a human maiden at all, but the female offspring of one of the lords of the underworld, Blood Chief. She grew up down there among the roots and the underground caves and rivers, among the dismemberers, the skinners, the cookers and eaters of flesh. She saw the creation of diseases and war, of pain and of sadness.

"Every moment of her existence there, the roof of her world leaked with the tears of the suffering above. Often a foul, sulfuric wind blew. At times the gales were so strong as to dismantle every structure erected there below. She had a job, one task for life: to separate the wheat from the chaff. Her fingers were bloody from going over and over every morsel of existence that fell into the underworld and separating any healthy grains from their crusty outer casing.

"At regular intervals, she would carry baskets of chaff to the underworld river of the dead and dump the husky residue into it to float downriver. Her life was an endless chore of inspecting, introspecting, separating, cleansing, and dumping, an utter recapitulation of every expended moment in creation.

"In order to walk to this river and dump her loads, she had to pass by a tree that it was forbidden to touch. On one trip to the river carrying her heavy basket she noticed that the tree had sprouted small fruits that appeared like little heads or skulls. All of the eyes on the little heads were closed. Several journeys to the river later she noticed that one of the little heads was peeping at her with half-open lids.

"After several more journeys the eyes were open. And after a few more she heard a whistle. She approached the tree with curiosity and the little head feigned innocence. She decided she was going to ignore this tree, so as not to get into any trouble, but at random intervals while walking with her basket to the river, she would hear a small hoot from the tree even though there were no owls perched on the branches.

"She was certain that it was one little head, the one that was awake. All the others appeared fast asleep, not even fully formed. Some had eyelids that could not be separated. Others had no real mouths to speak of. But this one little fruit was a fully formed tiny head and she was certain it was peeking at her, observing her on her path to the river, to and fro, listening for her footfalls and calling out for her from time to time.

"Little Blood Moon began to think that the head fruit was playing the part of a trickster and she determined even more insistently to pay it no mind, but one day the little fruit spoke out to her plainly as she walked by.

"'Oopa tsst, hey girl,' said the little head fruit with wide-open eyes." Don Juan then blew a raspberry, blowing air between his tongue and lips.

"'Not only are you a pest, you're rude!' said Little Blood Moon as she walked on with her basket.

"The little head was taken aback. It resolved to try a different tactic on her return.

"'I don't mean to offend,' said the little head as she passed by. 'I'm stuck here for a time, just like you. Wouldn't you at least like someone to talk with while you finish your work?'

"'Finish? When will I ever be finished?' Little Blood Moon said.

"'All the more reason,' replied the little head. 'I could be your only friend down here.'

"Little Blood Moon walked over and sat down under the tree with her basket. No one had ever sat down on the roots of that tree before. She looked at her bloody fingers and sighed. The head fruit whistled a haunting tune and at last she felt some relief.

"'Tell me, why are you doing what you do?' asked the little head.

"'I select the parts of creation that don't work, and I do this alone so that my seeing won't be tainted by desires,' she said.

"'And what happens to what does work?' the little head asked.

"'It ascends somewhere else,' she said.

"'What happens to what doesn't work out?' asked the head.

"'The lords of the underworld devour it and the residue gets dumped into the river of the dead,' she said.

"'My fruit survived and sprouted from that. And you work beautifully. Why don't you take some of me and we shall go somewhere else?' the head fruit replied. 'Let them learn from their own disaster down here. Let the twice-dead fight it out or be engulfed by their own sewage. As long as they have someone to clean up for them, they won't stop and everyone will suffer for it. I would like to give you something for free and you can decide.'

"'If you could do that, it would be wonderful!' she said."

Don Juan stopped his story for a moment to gauge my reactions.

"You see," he said, "the tree was her secret friend and it gave her something special, just like you were given something when you played alone in your basement.

"The little head fruit spit out a seed into her palm and told her to guard it carefully, lest any being try to wrestle it from her. The little head said, 'I have given you a sign. When a man dies people become frightened of the bones, but one's essence is not lost.'

"Little Blood Moon took her basket and returned to her place of work, for she was now long missing. The lords of the underworld were all asking, 'Where is the girl who cleans for us and prepares our food?'

"When Little Blood Moon returned, they cornered her and demanded, 'What have you been doing, girl? Where have you been? Show us what you have in your hand.'

"When she showed them her hand, the seed had been absorbed and there was a glowing place, like a hole or an eye inside the palm. The lords of the underworld all cried out in fury, 'She has defiled herself!' But Little Blood Moon replied that she had never known the face of a man, which was the truth.

"'Take her away to the house of solitude and night!' the lords cried out. 'Make her tell what has happened to her.' But the girl refused, even though she spent all of her time now alone in the dark.

"'Send in the sharp knives to cut into her flesh. Then she will tell us!' shouted the lords. But the girl was used to cutting, separating the wheat from the chaff. She was accustomed to bleeding fingers and so even though they cut at her flesh, she did not tell.

"'Cut out her heart that we may taste it and thereby know what she has done!' screamed the lords of death. But the owls came to the girl and whispered a plan. They did not want to kill Little Blood Moon. Instead, they flew to the sacred copal tree, tree of the nectar of the brain of the gods, and there they formed a heart of dark red copal sap. They flew with it to the lords of death and said, 'Here is the heart of Little Blood Moon, which the sharp knives have extracted for you.'

"The lords demanded, 'Cast her heart into our fire that we may watch it burn and the secret design will be revealed to us!'

"The owls cast the fragrant copal sap heart into the fire and the smoke from it was so aromatic as to mesmerize all the lords and demons of the underworld. The smoke from the copal sap heart wafted and ascended into the upper world, which opened to receive a clean, sacred, blessing offering. At this moment of infinite chance, the owls flew to Little Blood Moon and lifted her up on their wings and with their flight in unison, they elevated her up, up, up into the world above.

"And that is how the lords of death were defied and defeated and life in the world rose to this level. It was a woman who tricked them, a young woman, and the blessings of the sacred aromatic sap copal." Don Juan made a gesture of taking off an imaginary hat and tipping it at me with respect. I giggled like a little girl.

After a moment of thought, however, I became very disquieted. "But that's no consolation, bringing life to this realm where everyone still has to die, where there is pain and suffering, taxation and struggle, and the only perpetuation of life is that of living on in one's descendants." I felt the extreme pressure of the tragedies I had experienced speaking through me as though I were a medium. I shocked myself by actually arguing with don Juan!

He dismissed my blurting outburst, but not my angst, and he smiled wistfully. "A noble sentiment. This understanding of being is exactly why you are here. It leads us to the second part of our tale, that of the sacred hero twins. You see, in our way of Seeing, the way of Seeing with Dream Power, a double being or a sacred twin does not die because it contains the capacity to split again, like the egg of an immaculate conception, and to emerge out of the sacred void as another version of itself or as the sacred marital couple, Ometeotl. Such a being is unique, male and female in one, and it cannot be destroyed."

I took a deep breath of anticipation as don Juan began again. "This is now the story of the hero twins who defeat death and go beyond their Earthly existence into a cosmic being. The primordial double female being of Little Blood Moon has a male aspect, a primordial double male being called the Hunter and the Jaguar Deer. Female Little Blood Moon is the lunar eclipse, the moon and the void simultaneously. Male Hunter and Jaguar Deer are the relentless skilled seeker and the ferocious yet gentle truth of wisdom.

"Now when the time was ripe for them to face a male death, they traveled down, down to the lords of the underworld Xibalba, from which their feminine aspect had escaped.

Although they fought bravely and wisely there and won each of their battles against the lords of death, still Death itself ruled. Seeing this sign in their hearts, they decided that it was time to die to Death, and they offered themselves up to the sacrificial fire, asking only that their bones be ground and cast into the river of the dead.

"There was a great celebration throughout Xibalba because Death had won a final victory over man. Then five days later, two fishermen appeared on the river in their reed boat. They came working miracles. They could burn down a house and raise it back up again. They could sacrifice other beings and even themselves in turn and then restore everything to wholeness.

"The lords of the underworld demanded that these fishermen be brought before them to work their wonders so that all could be amazed. So ecstatic was the mysterious resurrection dance of these two strangers that the lords of the underworld cried out, 'Wonderful! Marvelous! Now sacrifice us and bring us back in the same way!'

"And so the lords of death were sacrificed and they were not brought back. It was then that the fishermen revealed themselves. 'We are Hunter and Jaguar Deer, and Little Blood Moon is above. Death will never again be great.' And with that, all three of these beings ascended into the sky to become its void blackness and its luminous nature and its all-reflecting wisdom. And together they show the way and Dream the bridge for all sentient beings to cross and follow."

My heart pounded as I sat in silence. I almost lost my breath. Don Juan got up quietly and went inside the house to prepare some desert herbs for an evening tea. He had taken an ancient creation story and woven it into my life and then transcended that with our genuine evolutionary energetic quest, a map, a marriage, and the mystery of a new kind of hope. I was stilled with contemplation and let his words sink as deeply into me as the golden black of the desert sunset that now enveloped the landscape.

The following morning, still immersed in the tale, I engaged in the newfound favorite meditative task of raking the desert sand into clean, swirling, energetic language patterns and sacred symbols all around the house and then of having an early walk. Don Juan was up at dawn and he had already Seen and felt the signs of the day. The wind and the mood had changed. We would be going south, down, deeper into the desert, and we'd see if we could find a longtime acquaintance of his, an old medicine Dreaming woman. About this he would say no more.

I had a very eerie feeling about this strange change of the wind's direction and even more so when we arrived on foot in the small community where we would look for this woman. For one thing, the town was even more deserted than Yuma, if that was possible. Yuma was the site of the "Hell of the West," which is still standing—a deliberately remote hewn-stone prison from the days of the westward expansion that housed stagecoach bandits, gunmen, and outlaws. The prison was known in those days for its dark solitary cell where the prisoner would spend as much as a month underground in total darkness, in utter silence, on bread and water, often in 125-degree heat during the day.

I had visited this abandoned prison often with don Juan during my stays with him and I thought that I had seen all of Xibalba there, the underworld of the dead and of the living dead. Ha! I hadn't seen the half of it until that particular day when it came walking boldly down the street, right before my eyes, in the form of a tall, dark, elderly native woman wearing a simple black dress with a black head-rag turban and carrying a huge machete.

"Leaping lizards!" I said to myself as I watched her set up shop, boiling corn ears in a washtub set on an old oil drum filled with smoldering coals. She took severed cornstalks from a burlap sack and, with her machete, she chopped the remaining bits of stalk right off the ears with a whack upon an old wooden crate.

"This is the woman who has been whispering to you since you were a child," don Juan said softly.

"Oh no," I said, thinking that he was kidding.

"Oh yes!" he said. "Here she is. The old woman from the basement, the genuine article, the real deal. Welcome to Xibalba!"

I was dead with terror. Yet despite it, I couldn't help my childlike desire to walk a little closer toward her. She was in fact magnificent, lanky, muscular, and hard. She wheeled around and glared at me like a medusa, but her hair of snakes was all bound up in her head rag. She was really beautiful, so severe. I was in awe of her but I dared not take another step.

I didn't know what to do; she had me pegged with her gaze. I couldn't even consider a false move. I actually bent down and made a gesture of kissing the earth, at which she released me from her stare. She glared at don Juan, he glared at me, and then something of both of them burned right through me. I felt as though the light from their eyes went nova, lasering me into a new helix.

Everything that I was died in me at that very moment and what was left was a new weave. Perhaps I had always carried it and they just singed me down to it, or perhaps I received a transmission that day, or both. But whatever it was, it has remained with me, it has remade my destiny, and it has taken me into the awareness that began prior to and then exists as and beyond the Tree of Life itself.

We never spoke of that experience. It was as though the power of it transcended all words, concepts, systems, and frames of reference. After that day, though, don Juan and I continually made trips south, and over time, I inched closer to this fierce enigma of steamed and roasted corn. I came to understand that she was highly respected and feared. She was beyond archetypal and was viewed as a powerful medicine person by the limited cognition of everyone near and far. This was not a being anyone would deal with lightly.

It took patience and humility to come near her, very much like gaining the tolerance of a wild animal, but gradually she became accustomed to my presence, although there was never anything that could be taken for granted. I observed the terror and standoffish behavior she caused in everyone in the community when she was out and about. The locals approached her with caution, if at all. One of her town chores was the selling of the corn that she herself harvested and cooked, and those interested in procuring some of it approached her like little children already holding out the exact amount of money required in their hands, as if to avoid any dialogue or need for her to make change. Just pay what you owe, exactly. That is all.

The corn was some of the best I'd ever seen. Huge, long, wide succulent ears, expertly roasted or steamed. Men had the most difficulty purchasing it; when in her proximity they actually seemed to lose their tongues at her harsh glare. Young women faired somewhat better and occasionally managed a mumble and a well-brought-up smile. Nobody passed her bin, braizer, and steaming tub uninterested, however. When my moment finally came to draw close enough to make the appropriate introductions, it was over that washtub of steaming ears.

I approached unlike the others, not holding any money in my hand but very definitely not asking for a handout. I figured that if we were to have any dealings at all, they had to begin on a basis of freedom and mutual respect. She hammered me with her stare and looked me up and down as if to say, "Well?"

"That's some very nice corn," I began. "You have an extraordinary skill for growing or selecting it. I have seen you here before and it's always the most excellent quality, far superior to anything else around."

"And?" she asked. "Tell me something I don't already know."

"That's all I wanted to say," I gulped.

She smirked. It was the first time I'd seen even a hint of the most sardonic of smiles on her face.

"You're not from around here, are you?" she asked with a warning tone.

"No, I'm not, but I do stay in the area nearby now," I replied respectfully.

"What do you do?" she challenged.

"Nothing. I mean, I don't 'do' anything." I had no idea what to say.

"Well, I've seen you before, too. What are you up to here?" she retorted. "What are you doing with him?" she asked, jutting her chin toward don Juan. "Be honest."

I certainly had no breath for lies. I would never have even considered it, but it wouldn't have been possible anyway. She definitely had the advantage now, which was rather disorienting and disconcerting. "I'm learning about the medicine of Dreaming," I replied.

"Don't you already understand?" she insisted mysteriously.

"Yes," I agreed. I gasped and rephrased my reply. "I'm deepening that understanding with experiences. I suppose that I am here experiencing. Yes. That's it."

"There is more to it than that," she responded and handed me a steamed ear of corn, expecting me to reach for it.

I didn't. "I can't pay with money," I told her. "I didn't bring any of that with me. I am grateful for this, if you mean for me to have it for free. Perhaps I could help you with something instead."

"And what would that be?" She laughed openly and signaled me with her eyes to bite into the juicy, golden corn. It was delicious!

"What could you possibly help me with?" she urged me.

After tasting the corn, I blurted out, "Well, for one thing, I'd like to be able to cook corn like this. Maybe I could help you carry and husk it."

"Trade me a recipe then," she said.

"What?"

"Trade me one of your best recipes, of your design, and you can have that corn, and I'll show you how I grow, select, and prepare it. Come back here at five o'clock exactly and we'll take a walk to my house. You can give me your recipe there and I'll show you my cornfield."

The ominous moment arrived. There was no turning back. At 5 P.M., I was standing like an orphan waif on the corner. She appeared with her machete and off we went toward her home. She told me to call her Celestina. That was all she said. The walk to doña Celestina's house was quiet and it took us across a small wooden footbridge and past several fields of corn that all appeared to be dry-farmed. We walked in total silence for a long way and eventually arrived at a large field on the right-hand side of the road that she indicated with a movement of her machete was her own field.

We stepped across the barrier of scrub bushes into the rows of tall green cornstalks. She pulled back the tasseled husk from one very large mature ear to show me that its kernels extended all the way around in rows without missing even one single space, culminating with a final kernel at the tip from which the tassel sprouted. The colors of the kernels were like a rainbow within a cloud, concentrated in some areas and then dissolving in others, with infinite transitions.

"All of them grow this way, complete with kernels all the

way to the end of the cob," she said plainly. "When an ear grows this way, it's called the Mother Corn, and if you take your seed from only such an ear, over time they'll all grow like these. Look how huge and magnificent these are and how the colors vary. White shifts to gold and then turns reddish. In the next generations, the dance of colors will evolve and reconfigure like the clouds in the sky to form new patterns, different from those that are present in the seed I'll select."

"How do you get them all to grow so big?" I exclaimed.

Doña Celestina smirked again. "Well," she said, "it is true that once long ago, corn was much smaller." She showed me half her pinkie finger to indicate its original size. "But it has always been very potent, like the ancient Earth herself, and if you understand what to look for, and how to choose and combine, and if you select only the best examples for seed, then over time corn grows larger and larger, and more powerful and substantial."

"I've never seen corn quite like this," I said.

"This corn is very like I am," she replied cryptically. "Look, if you see a person with a fine horse, for example, notice the relationship. Is it one of mutual respect and love, freedom and powerful spirits, or is it a broken relationship of domination and ownership, a trained creature burdened by a petty master, harnessed, restrained, miserable, and possibly even whipped? Just as with a horse, all you really have to do is whisper to corn and it will start to respond, if you really admire it. There is even a medicine test for young women at puberty who must prove their capacity for regeneration by praying their cornfield into being. A woman who does not pass does not have the qualities that are being searched for. To bring freedom into being, she must be free herself.

"And now, I think you understand that I'm going to give you a test. This one will be a little bit tough, a little different. I'd like to see if you can grow whatever you are asked by the spirits to grow, in the same way that one might pray corn into being, and do so freely. There is an intent behind this, but it's not going to be revealed to you yet. For now, I'm just going to insist that you do it. Pray and Dream. You say you understand. If you don't, you had better not dare come to see me again. Begin by Dreaming that bridge on the road that leads to my field right here and then later I'll tell you what I'd like for you to do with that. Dream it and walk across it, over and over again. It's that simple. Come to town and see me regularly only to show me how your Dreaming is going and then bring me what is on the other side of the bridge when you cross it. I'm not interested in anything else about you for the moment. And I'm not going to take you on farther to my house today. Instead, I'm going to leave you in my field. I want for you to smell the corn pollen. When you feel totally saturated with it, walk back across the bridge and go your way."

"Don't you want the recipe you asked me to share with you in exchange for this trip to your field and the corn you gave me?" I inquired, totally mystified, meek, and taken aback by her forcefulness. She was as strong when she spoke as when she was silent.

"Your Dreaming is the recipe I'm asking you for. It is one of your best. I'm not going to tell you just yet why I am asking you for it. Now go."

And with that, doña Celestina moved like a strong wind through her field, harming nothing and carrying the large machete at her side. She disappeared in a southwesterly direction heading toward what I could only suppose was her house somewhere off in the distance.

Practice Two

Dream Your Bridge and Walk Across It

1. This is an energetic crossing practice, a multidimensional practice that will carry you to the next level and into the infinite possibilities of benevolent intent and being. Begin by intending to see a bridge in Dreaming. Dream that same bridge over and over again each night.
2. Now awaken within the Dream to become lucid, fully aware within that Dreaming, fully cognizant that you are Dreaming, and capable of acting with awakened intent.
3. Lucidly examine every detail of the bridge and intend improvements, such as stability, beauty, environmental aesthetic harmony, and cleanliness if need be.
4. Lucidly intend a benevolent golden light surrounding the bridge.
5. Dream that you cross the bridge, fully awake in heightened awareness, walking easily and lightly all the way to the other side.
6. Search for versions of this bridge in the waking world and find them. You will be guided to them by your own energetic body, in the same way a homing pigeon is guided.
7. When you have found your bridge in the waking world, first honor it quietly, privately, and then walk across it in exactly the same manner as you walked across in Dreaming.
8. Do this often.

Bon voyage.

3

Evolutionary Revolution

When I first crossed the bridge in Dreaming, I could see ceremonial and evolutionary warfare on the other side. The ritual war was waged by the living and the dead. The purpose was "to be or not to be," and to realize or not to realize the original intent of creation. Upon recounting my first perceptions of these experiences across the Dreaming bridge to don Juan and doña Celestina, they immediately shifted their teaching stances with me and started to toughen and train me in the tools and tactics of genuine energetic and spiritual warriorship. My time with them became a rigorous boot camp filled with multidimensional obstacle courses, priority tasks, and sacred security clearances.

First, I started trance walking and running. The Yuman-speaking natives along the Colorado River all had individuals that they called Spirit Runners, persons who could run night and day for two, three, possibly even four days straight on minimal water and dried meat. These individuals had once served a vital purpose as the message relay system between peoples before and during the Spanish explorers. The male puberty initiation had consisted and still did consist, in part, of four days of trance running. I preferred to walk vigorously but I trained to run a bit as well, in silence, and soon I was able to enter a focused walking trance that Olympic athletes call "the zone," the sought-after state of optimum efficiency and excellent ability that allowed me to walk rapidly as much as fifteen to twenty-five miles straight on a daily basis, with only intermittent thoughts, no food, and little water.

Additionally, I was assigned the task of impeccable cleaning preparations for sacred ceremonies. I undertook the chores of cleaning: floors, clothing and ceremonial cloths, walls, windows and sacred mirrors, altars, tables, the ceremonial spaces, ritual serving items, healing stones, herbs and feathers, and, by offering sacred aromatic essences and smokes, even the air itself. From this I graduated to raking energetic designs in the perfectly cleansed sand outside the ceremonial spaces and then selecting certain items required for the specific ceremony and particular energetic work. From there, I went on to preparing and cooking some sacred concoctions and essences for the ritual participants and the energies. Then I began actually receiving the ceremonial energies into my body from a state of prepared emptiness and commenced designing elements of the ceremonies.

I began to arrange and blend magical configurations of energy, sacred substances, and space for empowerment and transcendental effects. I explored sacred geometry and architecture, direction, color, vapors, light, essences, music, rhythm, movement, chant, and invocation. I also studied a form of medicine song that does not have words. The words and melody of this kind of song come from the Twilight Language of Dreaming; they are understood only by the power of the Dream, which is called in with the singing.

Don Juan then advised me to deepen and lengthen my silences and to "empty my throat of all preconceived notions" in preparation, so as to be a vehicle for energy. Likewise my head and my womb had to be emptied as well. I undertook a period of voluntary celibacy in combination with endless days and nights of disciplined, blessed silence. If ever my mind began to wander rather than to receive energy directly, either don Juan or doña Celestina would appear as if out of nowhere and snap their fingers. During these days and nights I functioned entirely without any artificial noises or false electric lighting and there was always a Dreaming task when I went to bed at night, a task admonishing me to dive deeper into the work that I was doing and into what I was not-doing.

Beyond this, they both encouraged me to foster a solitary nature. Don Juan asked me to observe the behavior of the canyon pumas who never had any company and always hunted alone, elegantly. I did so, on my own, following their nocturnal tracks in the early daylight hours. Each of my mentors deliberately presented themselves to me as an archetypal solitary being and they asked that I be in the world but not of it, wherever I was, Seeing patterns in life and in cognitive agreements, and Seeing into energy directly. I followed don Juan's example and took to sitting alone in one of his favorite haunts, Lutes Casino, a nineteenth-century-period pool hall where one could view every aspect of life that straggled in from the hot desert, from the comfort of the air-conditioned shadows. No place on Earth has ever told me more about humans.

The task of crossing the bridge in Dreaming was a nightly proposition that I followed, and I was also instructed to "dig." I was spurred to uncover what lies beneath and behind all things without violating, destroying, or contaminating in any manner. When I was "deep enough," as my mentors put it—when I was ready—don Juan and doña Celestina then began bringing me items of ritual warfare, bones and dried skins, knives, ancient carvings and such. They would ask me to hold the bone, wear the skin, brandish the knife, or touch the carving. And then they would ask me, "Tell me, what is the story of that?"

They sent me down so deep that I could actually see the dead walking around like the living and talk with them about their battles and messages. I could do this soberly as if it were a natural thing while I went about my daily nonordinary business. The locals became somewhat wary of me then and steered clear of me for a time. I started to gain a reputation as a person with "medicine." Even after their instincts sensed that this energy was very benevolent and ultimately meant them no harm, some still remained quite apprehensive and tentative for a time. But they eventually warmed to me.

I could genuinely hear the undertones in every word spoken or left unspoken. They would all sink like stone into water, down into another level of communication and consciousness. I could pierce their delusions and slice through them like a hot knife through butter. I could illuminate my vision of the depths and see the treasure within different levels of being.

"Don't be afraid of it," don Juan would say to me. "This is a part of what you are."

One night I awakened into Dreaming to find myself outfitted for war. I was dressed like a ninja or a member of the Special Forces, all in black with a black ski mask over my face and my head topped with a black beret. My footsteps fell silently and I carried a huge machete. Suddenly I found myself surrounded by jungle and tribal peoples, all moving in a dance of possession to the beat of their drums and enticing me to come closer. A fire ceremony was in progress deep within a clearing and those who wished to see the world to come would have to go into the fire.

There were two men that I spied within the throngs who were nearest to the central ceremonial fire. One was seated and guarding it as if he presumed to own it. The other one lay dead, rotting. The seated man was an ashen blond. He turned to welcome me as I approached the fire and without any remorse or hesitation I decapitated him on the spot, hacking him into bloody pieces with the machete. Then I mounted the second man, who was a brunette, the one who was lying dead, and with tremendous excitation I began to undulate over his sexual organ. The fire spread until we were engulfed in its flames. He actually climaxed, as did I, and then he began to revive and recover his life.

I grasped his hand. We crossed the fire and stalked out of the jungle until we came upon an abandoned hut. I entered it. Inside the structure on a bare table I found an old military radio that was transmitting. Others from the primal fire dance approached the hut but they could hear nothing. I was the only one who could hear the transmissions or correctly decipher the messages.

When I awakened from Dreaming into my everyday awareness, I found that don Juan was already dressed for the day in his World War II military surplus khakis. Following the synchronicity, I walked into town alone later in the morning and easily homed in on several radios like the one I had Dreamed, waiting to be found on the shelves of the local Army-Navy surplus store. That night when I entered into Dreaming again, I had a glimpse of who or what was on the other end of the radio, but don Juan admonished me never to reveal that detail.

I couldn't help but be reminded of an experience I'd had as a girl traveling on a bus to visit my grandmother. On the long trip, I was seated next to a blind woman for half the journey. She held a multiband radio in her arms as though it were her lover. "When ever I am alone I can listen to my radio," she had said to me. "I love my radio. It tells me things you could never imagine. I have no one in my life. My family doesn't understand me. All I have is my radio, forever." She had said this honestly, and it had left an indelible mark on me. Now, I was faced with the radio.

"As the ferocious woman warrior I can See you're going to be," don Juan said to me the next day, "it will be appropriate for you to learn some things directly from Celestina de la Soledad, which means Celeste of Solitude or Solitary Celeste in English." Don Juan made this comment on the afternoon that followed my Dreaming, as we continued along the twenty-mile trek to her house. I was still thinking of the radio.

"I don't envy you having to stay there with her, but she will take you very, very deep," he went on. "She has a hard, clean edge, that one, and it will do you good to hone your own with it. You will sharpen her as well, so it's not all for nothing that she does this. It's not as though she gets nothing out of the deal, taking you in. But just remember this, that no matter what you learn from her, and mark me you'll learn well, ultimately you're not like her. She'll never own you, and you won't owe her when it's all over. She's aware of that and if you really live your truth, she won't feign otherwise. Not everyone has that advantage. Be mindful of it. You're simply not going to become what she is. That is all. There is no judgment in that. It's just so. You have your own path. Don't forget that, don't ever forget that," he said.

"I never will," I promised.

Doña Celestina's home was beyond the footbridge that I Dreamed so often. When I finally saw it, it lay at the outskirts of the small town we had visited, which was actually on the Mexican side of the border. The area was so deserted that there were no border markings or any kind of disputes, not even over water because there wasn't that much to contest. To live in this area one had to sink a well for water, which could be found in odd places, and this was not particularly conducive to town planning.

The house was solitary, small, and austere, a rectangular adobe construction with a kitchen, altar room, sitting room, and bedroom in the front, and several more bedrooms and a rustic bath in the back around a central patio, where the well water and the ceremonial fire pit could be accessed. I was given a bedroom in the back area when I arrived and it was understood that would be my room whenever I visited. The immediate sense I had of the place was that of a convent without the influence of Christianity.

There was nothing around except fields, mostly dry-farmed maize. You couldn't even see the nearest house, although there was one about a mile away within a stand of mesquite trees. It was a couple of miles to town. As for wildlife, there were occasional deer, rabbits, and coyotes, hawks, quails, grackles, crows, ravens, and turkey vultures, a colorful hummingbird now and then, and rattlesnakes and lizards, and, as I later learned, even a very few mountain lions that dwelled in the nearby dry water canyons. Jimsonweed, creosote, and ephedra were the most abundant wild desert plants, all of which have medicinal value. The bean of the mesquite is edible and there was plentiful native corn. Some of the neighbors kept bees. Mostly, it was totally silent except for the birdsong.

"Why do you live alone out here so far from the town?" I asked doña Celestina the first night of my stay with her as I was unpacking my rucksack. The isolation of the lone structure gave me a creepy sensation at first. The dim candlelight flickered on the bare walls.

"Do you think I'm too old and frightening to be alone?" she challenged me. "Does it scare you that in fact the older I get, the more independent I become and the less company I seek? While I'm strong, this is certainly what I prefer. Oh, and I get visitors out here." She jutted her jaw at me and lurched forward in the shadows. "I live far from the town because I can't stand the way that socialized women are taught to behave. I see through all that now. It's pure puny crap. Energetically, they're like enslaved children chained at the womb in a dungeon. All most of them know how to do is make more of themselves. At best, they're accomplished. Very few can cure, or do more. Some can clean up and sew well like convicts rehabilitating in jail, and so they're vain. Many just become shoppers and cooks and all they want is for everyone to eat up!"

I smirked. Doña Celestina was even more dark and misan-thropic than I had anticipated.

"You think that my view is odd, don't you? I'm not joking. Is there no end to the appetite? While you're here with me I hope to show you that I'm one of the very few women walking around with a clear head. I'm getting stronger. What about you? I don't care a damn about your unholy idea of me, mind you, so forget that, but I would like for you to absorb some of what I've learned from experience. Let's start with fucking," she said bluntly.

I was ready for that topic.

"All you young girls, you young women and even some older women who ought to know better—all you ever think about is how to get a pecker inside, how to make a baby, or how to get a man to do whatever you want. Your disgusting education revolves around how successful you are at that or how hard you have to work for it. There is no thought given to the fact that having a baby can kill. It's not something to be taken lightly. In many cases there is just no need for it. Most children conceived are ordinary in the extreme because the intent that conceived them was flimsy. And let's not even talk about the numbers!

"Women aren't taught about pleasure apart from the act that will cause conception, or apart from the pleasures of con-sumption, or of money and the so-called advantages it buys. Then they teach this to their offspring. They live like scavengers, victims, and dependent kept things. They aren't taught about their own power, that they can do for themselves, about the fact that almost everything on Earth that is of the flesh comes from them now. They aren't admonished to consider the joy and the suffering that little detail encompasses. They are totally attached, slaves who breed slaves. They understand so little of mature love. It's all about parenting, even parenting their part-ner and then marrying their child."

I had to sit down on the edge of the bed and I laughed nervously from horror. She was just so dead-on and relentless, threatening. I was about to pee myself from fear and hysteria.

Doña Celestina grimaced and looked at me as though I were crazy for a moment. "What, you think this is a party? You think I'm joking? Are you nuts? Look around! Look at the mess that life on this Earth is and sober up!" She walked out of the room and left me trembling at my own thoughts.

Doña Celestina's home was another place entirely at night. Once all the candles were blown out, it seemed to fill with a watery energy and become a bottomless well. The areas around all the edges softened and almost disappeared; they expanded immensely with fluidity, rippling like large sponges living at the bottom of the ocean. Owls would come to perch in the nearby shadowy mesquite trees and their rounded tones would float down into the patio like enormous descending bubbles.

I eventually followed doña Celestina into her altar room where she did work by candlelight late into the night. She was seated at a heavy, bare wooden table going through a pile of dried roots that appeared to be American mandrakes. She looked up at me and motioned for me to take a seat in a rough-hewn straight-backed chair across the table from her.

"The war you Dreamed is genuine. The adversary is any part of our being, living or dead, that falters from the task of originality in a cowardly delusion that keeps us from reaching the ultimate intent of all this," she said, motioning out onto the patio toward the sky. "It is a war from within, a war with the petty, ignorant, misinformed social self, and very few of us have the guts to stop suckling at the poisoned tit and fight it. It doesn't matter that all are dying and mutilating themselves with the cure. It's no good trying to convince the cultural consensus. It's like talking council diplomacy with an infant or a bully, and these are what our petty natures can be. Deep down, such nature is just a big, angry, poor baby coward that doesn't want any change that's not in its limited favor. It can accept no concept it can't reflect, nothing it hasn't heard of with its pea-brained, self-worshiping mind.

"I know, you're thinking that no one has ever spoken to you this way before. Who thinks and talks like this, after all? I can tell you that as a young woman I was a practicing midwife for a time, and I have seen all the stupidity there is to see! Now that I have grown and I am much older, I like to think of myself as a wiser woman who is a midwife for life moving toward its transition, toward a quality evolution, not into the senseless assembly line of pointless reproduction and consumption. Reproduction, you see, means making more of the same and it breaks the upward evolution if there is too much physical consumption because of too much carnal birth. Birth should be at the most auspicious replacement-level only. Ach! I've had about enough of the same old tedious repetition, haven't you? As with anything, if you make too much of it, it eventually suffers in quality, and that is definitely what we have among the human race. Oh, some of them masquerade in more attractive costume and their teeth last a little longer, but look at the ultimate results! On the inside they are just a house of cards!" She punctuated her statement by blowing the powdery dirt from the cleaned roots off the table and onto the cement floor.

"You're right! What can we do?" I gasped.

"It's very simple. Stop fucking. Stop the penetration." She inserted her right index finger into the hole formed by the encircled fingers of her left hand. "Both sexes can still have pleasure and reach a higher wisdom. Revolt. Evolve. Women have the reproductive and the evolutionary control and they shouldn't have to take it at the last minute with abortion or pills. There are other paths to pleasure, besides penetration. Women control the wombs. They can use that. They can put the brakes on and should be more selective. They have the capacity to focus on quality rather than quantity. Women will compete with one another for even the most pitiful dick on the planet. They need to stop doing that. If they would work together and support one another in this revolution, the whole world would turn around like that!" She snapped her fingers.

"I have young destitute girls who come to learn from me whenever they can find me. And when I get through with them, they are self-sufficient and dignified, and they understand how to empower women's councils. You can bet on it. They don't seek their power through a borrowed pecker, or merely through motherhood. These young women, educated and initiated or otherwise, are currently not the majority feminine population. So other women also need to see and change their way of being. They are very open to it, if caught at exactly the right moment, and you my dear have been caught at just such a time. There is no going back for you.

"I do not despise the male energy, quite the contrary," she went on. "However, it takes good females to bring good Earthly males into the world, if such is the need. Where do you think they come from, Mars? Perhaps a few. Right now, we certainly don't need to make more. We need to make better, or not at all. Sexuality is not intended only to be domination and surrender. And love is a call to ripen. Neither imply the necessity of wanton reproduction and endless ejaculations, especially not under less-than-optimal conditions. We have an obligation to seek completeness and that is not achieved simply by halving ourselves into pair bonds. Humanity is chained to a carnal agreement, which can be broken, or evolved.

"The male doesn't need to be satisfied," she clarified. "In fact, any high-quality courtesan will tell you that to satisfy them totally is the worst thing one can do. Then they become complacent.

Males need to strive, to go on heroes' quests and warriors' vision quests, and undergo rites of passage that earn them the right to be males, not the boys with potential that their mothers brought them into the world to be. And not all women are born to be mothers. Some were designed to be evolutionary consorts. Mothers are the favorites of boys, but the evolutionary consort will always be the favorite of the autonomous male. It is only natural. Such a consort is endlessly challenging and stimulating.

"You are not going to be a biological mother," she said bluntly. "I can tell you that right now. Don't weep over it. You are missing nothing. Look for your happiness in truly mature, autonomous male and female nature, and even beyond that in the sacred, the unique marriage, the union of both as one being. You're wandering in a forest of little boys and girls housed in partially adult bodies. You find yourself in a field of flowers, all with underdeveloped sexuality. These are sexual cripples. And you are just waking up to the horror that this is the condition of almost the entire planet and you are not like that. So you feel very much alone.

"I am here to show you that one can live alone with strength and dignity. You don't have to be afraid of it. You don't have to huddle in a squat shack with a roof that is too low just so that you won't die alone, just because you are not one of these maimed partial creatures living with an illusion of false perfection. You are like a unicorn in a corral with mules and you do not have to be one of them. It takes courage to be unique. Dare to do it. Try it. We all die alone anyway. It is liberating to know that clinging to one another does not change the fact that death comes to meet each one of us as an individual instance. That is even a good thing. I wouldn't want anyone else's death. Would you? I'd like to take my own chances, thank you very much. Don't sell me anything from anyone else. And don't you buy it. It wouldn't be good enough for you anyway."

Doña Celestina had just taken my whole view of life from the cradle to the grave and thrown it into the garbage can. She was correct, though. It was liberating. What an iconoclast! However, I couldn't help but wonder what I was going to do with my life now that I was not going to engage in "what everyone else does." Somehow, through the shock, I had the revelation that I was staying with her there to begin to explore just that, and yet as don Juan had told me, I would not be a carbon copy of her, for I had my own path.

I lay thinking about it all night. In the morning I heard voices out in front of the house. I dressed and after serving myself some tea from the kitchen, I peeked out the door of the sitting room to see who was visiting. There were two wooden chairs placed outside under the mesquite trees. Doña Celestina was sitting in one of them, somber, and a man of medium build and short stature with wavy hair was seated in the other. He seemed to notice me peering at them from the doorway and motioned for me to feel confident and come outside. Doña Celestina turned to give me a hard glance but she did not seem to feel that I was intruding.

I had a hard time perceptually processing this man after her insights, but there was something I liked about him. Still, my feelings concerning him were very far from ordinary. He was middle-aged. He seemed jovial and intelligent and he had dark thick hair that was touched ever so lightly with gray. His eyes were very pleasant. They were sweet and reminded me of the color of warm molasses. He stood up and extended his hand to me. I shifted my tea cup into my left hand to accept his. The handshake was very sincere.

"I'm Carlo Castano," he said. "I went to see don Juan this morning and I heard all about you. I've just come from there. I thought I'd come and see for myself."

"See what?" I asked, genuinely curious.

Carlo smiled sardonically. He put his hand on his hip and imitated my tone. "Why see you, of course, make your acquaintance, if you don't mind." His inflection was comical. "I feel better now that you're here."

"I certainly don't mind." I wondered why I would. "It's very nice to meet you," I added, sipping my tea.

"Do you have a name?" he nudged.

"Merie Madelyn," I said. "My friends call me Merilyn."

"That's lovely. How about if I call you Mem, something just between us?"

"Yes, all right." His English definitely had a touch of an accent.

"Carlo is on his way to Jalisco," doña Celestina said. "He's driving down toward Guadalajara today. There is a ceremony there that he's been invited to attend. It's a long drive and he'd like some company. He's inviting you to go with him. If you ride along, you'll be invited to the ceremony. You've already completely unpacked, haven't you? You can leave some of your things here and when the ceremony is completed, Carlo will bring you back—that is, if you'd like to go with him. If you do decide to go, just take enough clothing for a few days. You need to make a decision right now, because he has to get on the road again soon."

I looked at Carlo. He shrugged his shoulders hopefully. I thought about my bizarre night and the long conversation with doña Celestina. I gazed at Carlo and then followed my heart. What kind of a fellow was he anyway? "Just give me a moment to collect whatever you suggest that I bring," I said.

"You've made a good choice," doña Celestina said. "You'll benefit from the ceremony and the experience. You'll learn something and you'll be even more ready to work when you return. I suggest that you stop along the way and buy a good jacket. It will get cold if you go up into the mountains or stay outside in the high desert during the night. Oh, and Carlo, I am asking you to be on your best behavior," doña Celestina said cryptically with understated emphasis.

Carlo smirked and cringed. I went into the back to pack some slacks and blouses. Within a few minutes I had returned and Carlo had pulled his car around to the front of the house. The passenger door was open wide and he was standing outside it waiting for me. I got inside his vehicle and he shut the door gently. When he came around to enter his side and start the ignition, he gave me a smile, a wink, and a sigh of anticipation.

"I think you're really going to enjoy this," he said, and we started away.

Carlo didn't talk much about himself during the drive and I didn't tell him much about myself either. For me, it was enough that he was acquainted with and trusted sufficiently by don Juan to be told of my whereabouts. Carlo liked to be read poetry aloud when he drove long distances. He had come prepared, so I looked through the collection he had in the backseat until I found something that suited my taste. I selected verse by St. John of the Cross. I had completed a double major in Comparative Religion and Philosophy and Language while at university and so I came by my choice honestly. I thought that particular selection would be more passionately read by me aloud, as nothing is worse than listening to a monotonous rendition of beautiful poetry.

Carlo seemed to be surprised but pleased with my choice. He listened carefully as I measured the musical tempo and the heart-filled explorations of exquisite ecstatic flight and vision. Ecstasy was my area of emphasis in the study of global spirituality. Women are often repressed in religion, but the sincere ecstatic experience is one domain where all will stand back and let the woman have it. I was quite in my element reading the verse and actually rather impressed with his good taste in prose and thought. Finally the verse carried me away. Carlo would comment from time to time. His command of his second language, English, was impressive. He seemed fairly gifted in his own tongue as well and gave me the distinct impression that he was quite familiar with a wide variety of regional Spanish and Latin American accents. He was a very good mimic and focused in his conversation, highly comical, and most entertaining.

He asked me if I could sing, too. I do, but I declined to do so that day, for I couldn't think of an appropriate song for the road. We were a little giddy from our enthusiasm. Doña Celestina was correct: it was a very long drive and I could see why he had requested the company. Slowly the Sonoran Desert began to be flanked to the east by the bluish mountains of the Bacatete Sierra mountain range, and after that the foliage became more lush and the air more fresh.

It was about a twelve-hour ride to Guadalajara but Carlo told me we weren't going all the way down to the city. Instead we were going to turn east near the mescal territory and head for a small Huichol town by the name of Tuxpan. From there we would all go to the ceremony. We stopped in the very pleasant town of Tepic for a bite to eat in an outdoor restaurant near the town square, right before we headed east. Carlo said that they had a good public market, so we leisurely walked there afterward to procure a warm woven jacket as doña Celestina had recommended. We saw a Huichol shaman standing near the herbal section of the market. When we got back into the car, Carlo started to tell me a little about where we were going.

"I don't want to say too much," Carlo began. "Do you know anything about the Huichol Indians and their ceremonies?"

"Not that much," I replied. "I certainly know enough to be respectful."

"Well, you may learn quite a bit. Everything will depend on the shaman, as to how much they let you see and participate," he said, "but I'm going at the shaman's invitation, so I think this could be a very fortunate experience for you."

"Thank you for asking me along," I replied sincerely.

"The ceremony won't begin until tomorrow and we will arrive very late tonight, so if you like, you can just relax now. I feel a surge of energy and we'll make the rest of the drive without incident."

It was very late, past midnight, when we pulled into the town of Tuxpan. The shaman, don José, greeted us and invited us up to his compound. The Caliguey, the central ceremonial hut of the village, was active and the flames of the original fire spirit, Grandfather Fire Spirit Tatewari, burned within it, tended by another shaman. Don José already had some pallets laid out for us. He seemed to have been anticipating us both, which I thought was unusual. Carlo lay down to rest and as he did so, don José pulled me aside.

"You know," don José said, "if you want to participate, you'll have to have a Dream and tell me everything you see in it."

He didn't tell me what kind of Dream I was supposed to have and I knew better than to ask. Don José merely indicated that I was to take my place on my pallet and rest now. I fell quickly into Dreaming. Carlo was snoring softly on the pallet beside mine, laid out on the earthen floor under a thatched ramada outside the shaman's hut.

I awakened into Dreaming to see thousands of disembodied eyes all around me, peering at me from every direction. It was so startling that I jumped up off my pallet and ran to the Caliguey. The fire from within was the only light in the village. Grandfather Fire was being kept company by several younger shamans, several older shamans called Mara'akames, and don José, the oldest of them all. Don José looked up at me standing in the doorway and motioned for me to come to the fire.

"Did you Dream?" he asked. "Tell me everything you saw."

"Oh the agony of all those disembodied eyes!" I blurted out. "I think they were ancestors watching me, watching all of us."

Don José looked at me approvingly and nodded his head. "She can participate," he announced to all present. And so it was.

The ceremony for the men was going to take place within a sacred cave, a place of feminine power like a womb space for the male shamans. Another group of shamans, young novices, and medicine women were traveling to a place of male power, a sacred mountain called Wirikuta. I was to be taken to the mountain. In the morning, the two groups of ceremonialists were preparing themselves for their trips to the sacred sites. Carlo had been invited to join the group of males going down into the cave.

"Don't be frightened, Mem," he said. "Don't worry. You can trust this. We'll each receive what is required. I'll take you away after it's all over." He looked at me firmly in the eyes for a long moment to let me understand that come what may, he meant what he said. We went our ways with last glances at each other.

My group heading to the mountain was already piling into several trucks. The travel to both of the intended ceremonial destinations, combined with all the required final preparations and then the specific ceremonies enacted there, would last for approximately three days. The two ceremonies of the sacred cave and the sacred mountain would occur concurrently. Both groups were going to travel part of the way on foot as a penance. For our group, the foot travel would begin when we reached a sacred river that we'd cross after receiving a blessing from the Mara'akame, don José, who was going with us. From that crossing at the river, we would proceed toward the top of the sacred mountain, passing through peyote fields along the way. The shaman would gather an abundance of the peyote cactus—or *hicori*, "tracks of the magical deer"—and then all of us were going to climb up to the top of the peak hauling it, and at a designated site, we were to make offerings.

Our group drove almost without stopping the first day and night and we crossed the river early at dawn the next morning. There were many prayers and confessions offered among the Huichol at the banks of that river before don José painted their faces with sun symbols made with a natural yellow paint freshly pounded from a local root. The sparkling peyote desert appeared like no other. The scrub there was brawny with low rambling thorny bushes, surrounded by pebbles near their roots. Each bush had its own small territory and many twinkled with a ring of little thornless cacti nestled flush with the ground underneath their branches, almost like fairy rings. The imbedded circular heads of the sacred cacti ranged in diameter from about one-half to three inches across. They were bluish greenish gray and naturally pie-sectioned into five, seven, or occasionally even more spongy little segments with a tuft of hair in the very center of each button.

I stood openmouthed, leaning over to look at a nickel-sized button from which I actually heard whispering, humming, or crackling like a telegraph wire or a transistor radio. Don José came over to me and patted me on the back. "You're just like me," he said. "Sensitive. All you have to do is smell their little hairs. You just smell their pollen and up you go!" He pointed his index finger to the sky.

He then gestured toward the sacred mountain in the distance. It was a huge jagged blue peak with a distinctly perceptible natural stone formation like a throne or a slab, which appeared to be covering an entrance at the summit. A huge blast of wind rushed out of that very spot and from miles away it pounded me almost instantly as though the hermetically sealed doorway into another dimension had been opened, just as soon

as I gazed upon it. That place was sentient and it focused on the
feeling of being touched by my eyes with awareness. The wind
gusted and grabbed my attention like a choke hold at the throat.
It had me. That particular point on the mountain cemented my
gaze deliberately. It was definitely the living abode, the foot-
stool, or the gateway of a spirit. I felt something ooze down my
throat and squeeze at the pit of my stomach. Whatever it was
held me transfixed.

Then the wind receded and the sun shone from behind an
evaporating morning cloud. The colors on the mountain
changed to a pale rosy shade of stone. I could breathe and move
my eyes. Don José was walking through the fields with a long
stick, pointing out the tracks of the magical deer to younger
Huichol men who scrambled to dig the small cacti out. There
was a twinkle in the old shaman's eyes as he looked at me from
time to time, a twinkle that matched the playful, impish mood of
the sparkling peyote and the morning breeze that now flirted
with us from out of nowhere.

Huge burden baskets filled with the conical peyote cacti,
roots and all, were loaded onto the backs of the younger
Huichol men. I have no idea how I climbed that sacred mountain with those men and women. The next thing I knew, we were
all at the top and the wind was rushing down. From our eagle-
eye vantage point we scanned the fields of peyote. The wind
shouted in my ears unceasingly. It surrounded me and whipped
around us. Its motion and light play projected momentary perceptions onto the blank fields of my vision below. I was as high
as a kite and I have no explanation for how I got that way.

I don't know how I got down the mountain either! I don't
remember climbing down after the first step or two. The next
thing I knew, it was night and we were all sitting around a big
sacred fire. We were completely outside of linear time. There
were no transitions. The Huichol were chomping away on pey-

ote cactus and singing and I could understand everything they said in their language. I laughed at the exact moment everyone else did, every single time, without the slightest verbal cue.

The Huichol told me then that I was having conversations with God. It seemed like a good explanation. All of the extraordinary experiences were shared and were validated. No one was imagining anything. There was no need to. Imagination wouldn't have been nearly as interesting or as profound. There was this circle of light around everything we perceived as though we were inside a bubble that was taking us on a journey to exactly where it had designated we would go. Time and space were only in context within the bubble, which could rearrange itself instantly, at will, without causing disorientation. Nothing was linear. Nothing repeated itself, and yet there was a circular quality.

We were joyful, inspired, enlightened, and wondrous, and we were filled with longing all at the same time. I was so alive I ached, and so detached and liberated I floated gleefully. There was an awareness that all moments come to an end and a sense of timelessness and eternity paradoxically. Time was malleable and responded to intent, but then just relaxed of its own will and let itself be carried away like a sailboat in the wind or like a hawk soaring freely on a newfound thermal current.

It was possible to move the awareness in any direction, forward or backward, above, below, within, or around and around and to touch anything in spirit, no matter what the distance. This touch might occur after a period of traveling with the awareness or calling with the heart and mind, or sometimes, it would simply be instantaneous, simultaneous with the intent.

I awoke in the morning after the all-night fire ceremony without ever having gone to sleep. The fire was out without ever having burned down. All I felt was love. That was everything and nothing. It was the distilled essence. There was no condition for it and no needed object of it. There was no anchor for it in time or space. I had no words, no thoughts, no hopes, no expectations, no desires. Life was a surprise and I wasn't fooled.

I didn't think I'd ever see Carlo Castano again, or anyone else. I was sad and liberated, and thus joyful. I didn't think I'd ever eat again, or go to the toilet again, or brush my teeth . . . and if I did, I wasn't going to believe any of it. That was my determination. These things did occur, but I kept to my promise not to believe. They were illusory and temporal, not an all-encompassing intent. In the case of Carlo, however, I couldn't help but enjoy being with him.

Our raggedy band had a long drive back from the sacred mountain Wirikuta. The peyote-laden burden baskets followed by the Huichol themselves were piled into the flatbed trucks. I sat in the front seat with the old shaman don José. We seemed to rate this seat next to the driver, a middle-aged, husky Huichol man. Don José sat there because of his elder shamanic status, and because he had made many a pilgrimage entirely on foot, and I sat there, perhaps, because I was the only one who had never conceived of making such a journey before. The world was not real. We were not real. We simply did what was natural.

If ever I have to say that I loved Carlo Castano from the first moment I laid eyes on him, I suppose that now is the time to do it. There was something about him being one with that cave at the same time that I was on top of the sacred mountain that made his presence forever indelible in me. I could see him, feel him, trust him, in essence touch him, like a mist or a cloud or a floating pool, as though the whole expanse of sky and our entire existential realities were nothing but the vaporous opening to that deep sacred cavern, and my being, my heart did nothing else but receive that open doorway upon the shimmering summit of spirit. Everywhere I looked there was void filled with his presence and fragrant vapors. My sight, my essence was as wide open as the sky and every direction was a different, even an infinite variation of that same intended destiny, always new, never lost, filled with endless possibilities. How can one explain such things? It is not possible.

We came to the determination that it would be very difficult to talk about what we had experienced. Words were not sufficient. It wasn't something that "knowledge" could encompass or express. We could feel it. We could sometimes see it. We could move more deeply into it. We could go with it and intend toward it and we could communicate within it—but explanations were like clouds shifting in the sky, as impermanent as that and yet, for brief moments, as utterly tangible. Although he expressed to me what happened in that cave a million times plus one, each time it was something different, ancient and new, and all are true. There is no way to "know" what it was. There is no history for it. Likewise, I have never recounted my experience on the mountain the same way twice.

Carlo used to say, "We've never lied or made anything up. We've never even come close to describing it. Can't we work together on this? We don't even know what it was ourselves!" That was the succinctly put truth of it.

When our group had returned to the village, Carlo was already snoring away in one of the huts at the canyon's edge. His group had been back for several hours. I settled into that grouping of huts myself. Clouds were drifting right past the rim of the canyon, through the abyss. They were traveling through open hut windows and beneath the ramadas. The old shaman don José gave me a hand-woven blanket to roll up in and soon afterward, all of existence dissolved.

In the morning, I found a book on Tibetan Dreaming practices, called Dzog Chen, that Carlo had put near my head as I slept. It had been there by me most of the night, and it was intended as a silent gesture from him. I realized that morning that I had discovered something very profound. Yet I couldn't express it. Evolution in our understanding—moving toward experiencing the essence and the ultimate intent of creation and existence—means a new conception of what it is to be alive, to love, and to die. Nothing can be the same, not even time. The perceptions and the possibilities of the whole of our manifest being have to awaken to this ultimate intent, and change upon the awakening.

Practice Three

Dream Quest

1. For this practice, you need to select a solitary mesa or a flat-top mountain. You must climb to the top and prepare to spend the night under the open sky, within a sacred circle of stones or a circle of ceremonial ash, which you circumscribe at twilight in an auspicious clearing with a good celestial perspective.

2. From the moment the circle has been prepared and you are within it, until dawn, do not leave the circle. Take care of all of your bodily functions beforehand and be conscious of your diet and beverage intake for several days prior to this offering, so as to give your body the best possible advantage. Eat and drink sparingly on the evening of the Dreaming.

3. Lie flat on your back within the circle wrapped in a warm blanket or bedroll and gaze with a soft focus up into the night sky until you enter Dreaming. Your head should be facing east.

4. The intent is set to receive energy and guidance from your offering. Hold this intent without wavering as your levels of awareness shift. It is helpful to visualize the head of a comet followed by its coma entering into your body from the sky through the crown of your head as you move more deeply into trance levels and the intended Dreaming.

5. Each time you awaken into or sink into a different level of awareness, reset your intent. Do this without exerting rigid,

obsessive control. Rather, let the depth of Dreaming and the force of pure intent sail you off into your timeless journey.

6. Feel the gravity and stability of the mountain and at the same time feel your being and the mountain as one, drifting into the infinite throughout the night.

7. In the morning, spend at least one hour in totally silent, grateful contemplation and recall the night's revelations before clearing away, eating, or starting the climb down.

4

The Tree of Life

Several weeks later, after my return with Carlo, I found I was still in the afterglow. I was spending the month alone with don Juan while doña Celestina took care of some business "clients" from Yécora, Sonora. Doña Celestina's clients were the local people from the region who needed her services as an "energetic intermediary." This work often required her complete and rigorous solitude, so that she could transform herself into the necessary presence prescribed for the task, via the summoning of her energy body and powers through Dreaming. I was not allowed to observe all the details of such a metamorphosis yet, as I was still learning to Dream deeply and precisely enough to approach the profound depths of what she would later reveal to me.

At such sharply transformational times in her work, I was told that it was better to stay clear of her, unless I was going to accompany her in acting upon the intent. She had instead given me a task that she called *mano que cura*, "the hand that heals," and she had sent me to don Juan's house with a specific Dreaming prescription. I was to Dream of my hands and allow a nurturing, pearlescent, milky energy to emanate from my fingertips. If any being came to me then, during my Dreaming, and in need of this energy, she had told me to suckle them with it by allowing the energy to be licked directly from the tips of my fingers.

I found myself sitting alone along one of the irrigation

canals underneath a tall eucalyptus tree one afternoon. I was gazing at my hands. They had started to weep in Dreaming and I had wrapped them in gauze and linen during the day, to protect them from the ordinary energies of everyday life. I lay down under the tree and crossed my hands over my heart. I closed my eyes and contemplated Dreaming. Then I rose and started to unwrap the bandages. My solitary existence insured that no villager had even noticed I had bound my hands. They were quite luminous and fresh looking once they were unwrapped.

It was getting dark and don Juan came ambling down the path from the village. I bunched all the bandages into a little pile and placed them on the roots of the tree. In the twilight, I had the strangest sensation that it really was not don Juan that I was seeing at all, not the being with whom I was acquainted, but something else. I sensed his approaching body as a kind of winged energetic being. There was a lift and a luminosity to his shoulders that I was unaccustomed to perceiving and a rippling light play of energy emanating at his sides that flowed from behind him, almost like a cape. I sat rapt in the vision of his approach.

He sat down under the tree and glanced at my pile of bandages. He smiled slightly and began to sing and whistle softly, something he loved to do while relaxing under trees. He was wearing his khakis, which glistened in the dusk, and he leaned his head back against the tree trunk to relax.

"This is the kind of place that a man, or sometimes a woman, comes to make an offering when they are ready to leave the hold that the Mother Earth has upon each one of us," he said, in a tone of mystical contemplation at the end of daylight. "That being may then continue the Earth walk as an upright free being for the rest of the time on Earth, but life will never be the same. It's really a male mystery . . . but you have the right kind of energy for it," he mused, "so I am going to talk with you about it.

"Someday, you are going to be in the same position that I am. You will find yourself independent of many of the trappings of Earth. You will not be attached to family, but rather peering into the vastness of an infinite love. You will not be tethered to the Earth, but you will still be walking about the paths here. You will not have debts or entanglements. You will have no illusions and few fetters. You will not need to own all the possessions that give life such an extreme material weight. You will see the illusory nature and ultimate impermanence of what everyone calls 'reality' and you will experience solid structures dissolving before you like sand sifted through your hand. Your world will not be routine. You will understand the why and the wherefore. Your daily awareness within will become the clear light of our simple, natural luminous nature. Even the body will become an illusion for you, and the world of those bound to limited knowledge and descriptions, machinations, and partial intent will become a world on the other side of a barrier of energy that others cannot cross.

"I want you to understand now that doña Celestina is not evil. Even though some might prefer a world without her, she is necessary to them. She's like a dark mother and for some reason, they need her. We've all had one, a dark mother, one way or another."

I laughed. "Perhaps she is the dark Anti-Mother," I suggested.

There was a faint smirk on don Juan's lips. "But we have other natures besides that child in the dark, born of a dark mother, and few of us ever find them," don Juan continued. "Most of us are terrified to let go of Mother. Yet not every aspect of Mother wants us. How can we fly freely and be initiated into a true adulthood, into genuine partnership and the sacredness of an autonomous marriage of love, wisdom, skill, and freedom, until we let go of our need to forever be her children?

"Some males undergo rites of passage that initiate them into true warriorship, which frees them energetically from being only a son to a mother forever," he went on. "Some women warriors undergo such rites also, and you are one who is going to do so. Most women undergo rites of passage to assist them and prepare them for becoming mothers, but as doña Celestina has already explained to you, pointedly, that is one step, one endless turn around and around the wheel of life that you are not going to make. You are going to be more like a warrior male and walk independently, without attachments. Or better yet, you'll be something new, a marriage of both, a new kind of medicine vessel.

"That will mean sacrificing and sanctifying your flesh," don Juan said firmly. "It is the only way to get outside of the bubble of the Earth agreement. Everything here exists within the womb agreement of the Earth, regardless of how priestly or how mundane, and it all begins and ends there, everything, that is, except the Celestial spirit, which transcends. Not every being has that kind of spirit. Most beings on Earth are like children or even animals and they are purely Earthly and underworldly. They have spirits, but the spirits are encased in two realms, the realm of the dead and the realm of Earth. Sometimes, as you have seen, there is not much difference between the two. They coexist. The main difference is that the living on Earth must have a body, a temple, or a form from the womb. The dead do not always have one and they do not have to have one. They may borrow or do without. Both realms ingest energy. But the Tree of Life and awareness consists of three sacred levels: the Underworld, the Earth, and the Celestial.

"When I say you will sacrifice your flesh, I mean that your spirit must be liberated from the placenta and the womb of the two-level existence. There is other energetic nourishment out there and other protection. There are realms beyond consumption and predation and bodies that are neither dead, nor made of organic flesh. As good as this all is here at the Earth level, at the summit of this two-level state of being, which is almost like a glass ceiling, the womb of Earth breaks the upright nature that ascends and devours the broken portion in order to feed the lateral expanse of creation and beings that exist within the womb of Earth. Yet a tall redwood tree cannot grow in a two-story building for very long, unless that building has a hole in the roof.

"These realms can work together, which is a high intent. However, as long as there is conflict and possessive misunderstanding, or if one's spirit is not willing or able to transcend the endless cycles of birth and consumption, dismemberment and consumption, and death and consumption, one will not attain the Celestial level. Among shamans, an ending of this conflict is essential. One offers up and one undergoes an energetic death and dismemberment, sometimes more than once, as an initiation practice for death and in order to proceed with the Earthly death. If something rises from that process, then that being is developing the capacity to transcend.

"Male energy has the capacity to transcend the womb of Earth like an arrow shot into the sky that breaks the bonds of gravity, or like an eagle soaring on high that does not often land, and when it does, it does not land on the ground but rather in a treetop or on a mountain peak. So may the energy of the sacred marriage within a being transcend the Earth, like the marriage of fire and water in a rainbow transcends the horizon. The transcendence requires a refined vehicle, made exclusively of light or of mind or of some other refined spiritual essence. In the case of a collective transcendence, a new feminine is required, an immaculate conception if you will, a new vessel that is the conception of another realm into which beings may emerge.

"In each of these instances, there comes a point of either a return to the familiar or a journey beyond. A decision is required and an empowerment. When the being reaches the limits of the Earth womb, it is palpable. The Mother Earth energy will struggle to keep everything within herself, for if she loses something, she loses energy and food for her children—but it can be done, and done with permission and done without harm. She will even give a boost to send something beyond herself, in the right situation. It takes a lot of energy to do that, and most beings simply don't have enough. Sometimes the Earth will make a being or two that have that capacity to go beyond her, for her own very strategic and transcendent reasons. You have that capacity. And I do.

"Understand that if a being leaves this agreement, the Earth Mother may get to divide up the leftover remains, but the most refined spiritual essence is gone forever from her grasp. It can never again be consumed as food, ever. This will cause profound feelings in life here. Earth life will struggle to hold on and consume and the essence will continue to drop its heavy load and refine beyond any clutches.

"To achieve such transcendence, one must love the spirit and love freedom more than one depends on the cycle of containment. In that way, if one acts accordingly, forcefully and gently, subtly, with wisdom and compassion, one accumulates even more energy that is not attached. This transmuted, less burdened energy can be translated into a freedom-generating way of being. This is easier to say than it is to do, but the life force cooperates.

"Many beings have weak backs when it comes to comfort or to giving up their familiar worlds, regardless of how enslaving they may be. Deep inside them, they capitulate. They dilute themselves and it creates conflict for them. Then they overreact with their strengths. Such beings cannot marry their own natures because they are not extracting a new essence that transmutes them all. Those beings may also have fears and extreme feelings of cyclical dependency. Yet if one with enough energy perseveres in the proper way, that being will eventually move out of all those realms in some mysterious and individual manner and reach the outer limits of Earthly dependency. That being will reach an internal state called freedom. At that point, it is possible to go beyond according to our individual artistry, instead of seeking to retreat into hibernation, habit, and flesh."

I looked at don Juan with some trepidation. I had every question possible at one level, and at another, I had none. I opted for none.

"I would like for you to find a solitary tree," he said. "Go and sit under it day and night. Sing to it, Dream under it, keeping in mind and in focus this three-level intent that I have shared with you. Bear your soul, weep, laugh, call out, dance if you'd like—and then wait. Wait and see what comes. Wait until something does."

I did as requested and selected an old mesquite that was one of don Juan's favorites. I went there day after day alone, and positioned myself underneath it in the morning so that I could watch the whole day pass. I always brought a little carpet with me to sit on and some tea and wholesome snacks. Indians on the reservation would smile at me occasionally as they walked by and they did not seem to find my continual presence there incongruous, as everyone was accustomed to seeing me around the reservation.

I ate my lunch under that tree and sang to it the way don Juan often did. I sang to the birds and whistled my medicine tunes. In the afternoons I gazed at the sandstone pillars against the invariably clear blue sky, reddish oblong silhouettes standing out strikingly, far off on the northern horizon. I relaxed and enjoyed. I sat so quietly that I often went into a trance and I'd forget all about the intent, or rather I'd release my fixation upon the intent. I felt a great deal of healing energy coming from that tree.

One beautiful late afternoon I entered Dreaming, passing the doorways between wakefulness, trance, sleep, and Dreams with full awareness. I Dreamed of a native man in khakis coming to sing with me under the tree. I Dreamed of Carlo Castano coming to bring me food. Suddenly, I realized that I was not alone under this tree! Something on the other side was casting open winged shadows across my shoulders. I turned around to look behind the trunk and I saw a small man standing there. The shadow was emanating directly from him. There was the appearance of a pair of nearly invisible, translucent, almost imperceptible wings on his back that cast the shadows, even though the wings themselves could definitely not be seen if one looked directly at his body. These were not luminous wings like those I had perceived around don Juan's body at twilight. These wings were shadows and the absence of light. This being turned around to look at me just as I looked at him. He feigned surprise.

"Hello," he said. "What are you doing under my tree?"

"I was going to ask you the same thing," I said, genuinely astonished. "And I didn't know that this tree belonged to any-one," I commented.

"Oh, but it does!" he replied, and his eyes widened like an owl's. He walked around to my side without invitation. He seemed a little drunk. I was apprehensive of him. "Allow me to introduce myself," he said, facing me. The winglike emanations at his back stretched out to their full length and cast huge shad-ows on the ground. Their expanse was elegant and impressive, exquisite. The shadows on the ground rippled and whispered to me like rustling leaves, or like the soft wind, and it was as though my mind were speaking, saying a name that I did not wish to repeat out loud.

I looked up from the ground in silence, stilled. This being wasn't quite solid, but barely enough so as to cause him to appear to be a man.

"Do you have any friends or family over here on this side of things?" he asked.

I was not going to give away anything to an apparition. I replied, "Just this tree."

"Well, I've been called to come out here before, and often. Usually I just send an emissary. I'm hardly ever interested enough. But for you . . ."

"Oh, I bet you say that to all the girls," I half joked, petrified.

"I don't think so, but we can play it that way if you like," he remarked.

"So what precisely makes me and this tree so special anyway?" I insisted. "Why do I get to be the 'lucky' one?"

"Do you mean you really don't know?" he asked.

That sounded to me like a trick question. "No, I don't know," I retorted. "Is that why you're interested?"

"Oh, I could think of a hundred thousand reasons, plus one, but yes, not knowing is very intriguing."

I felt something grab me then and lift me up, almost as though I were wearing a harness. The sensation was of being rapidly hoisted, back first. Just as suddenly, all of my physical, bodily awareness was gone. My luminous awareness now found itself not at the bottom of the tree at all, but rather at the top. What was before me there was not a shadowy being anymore, but something akin to a luminous doubled egg floating in front of me, a twin ellipse about the size of a human being. I had an extreme sensation of joy beyond anything I had ever experienced.

A voice from the luminosity spoke to me in my Dreaming language. "This is your natural, enlightened, formless awareness," the voice intended. "The beingness at the bottom is of the Underworld dead, and the trunk of the tree supporting your back is the pillar of the life of Earth. For you there is little temptation to remain in the lower levels; there is nothing left to pay, and very little enticement. When you are silent, when you Dream, when you See, when you circulate your energy around, when you depart from the form—this is the celestial place for you to come. On Earth there is a way forward for many, and yet the ignorance blinds them in divisiveness. For you there is no division, only cooperation."

I awoke back into my bodily awareness as the afternoon sky was changing colors. I was alone under the tree and I began to sing again. I was wistful not to still be at the luminous top, but I was joyful for the experience of it. I was happy to be experiencing such a beautiful afternoon, but I was saddened by the temporal nature of Earthly life. I was actually sorry not to see the little winged man anymore, but I decided that in this case, the temporal nature of existence and infinite diversity were working for me. I realized there was great wisdom in accepting that instead of clinging. I thought perhaps being too curious about him was a choice I ought not indulge in. I let go. If he came to visit me again that was one thing, but I was not going to go looking for him.

I remembered an Islamic saying that God created the desert so that he can be by himself, and another saying not from Islam, but just as wise, that both God and the Devil are equally at home in the desert. I had never had a trinity of simultaneous perceptions in my life. It was as though I had been on all three levels at once. I had feelings regarding each as if I had been three different beings or had lived three different lives as the same being, or had seen life with three eyes, each with its own identity.

Don Juan did not ask me about my experiences at the tree. It was obvious that I had encountered what it was necessary for me to See. I did take the opportunity to ask him some questions, though. The following evening while we were preparing some deer meat for dinner, I began my queries.

"Do you believe in destiny, don Juan?" I asked while I smelled the aroma of fresh strips of deer meat roasting over the open fire at the back of his house.

"I don't have to believe," don Juan said plainly. "This just is." He extended his arm with an open palm in all directions to encompass our periphery.

I watched him crouch at the fire while the flames leapt for the meat, casting a beautiful golden glow on his aquiline features.

"We are like pathfinders," he said. "We will go where others cannot. You may wonder about me—for example, why have I never truly married? I married Dream Power because the kind of marriage I was looking for on Earth did not exist. It did not come along in my life until now. This world is not the place for such unions. Everything here gets carved up for food." He turned the meat over in the fire. "Nothing reaches its ultimate potential here on Earth. Earth is fertile, holistic, abundant, and nurturing, yes, but she clings and she kills. She cannot take in everything, no matter how much knowledge she amasses. There is such a thing as a spiritual journey beyond what she holds and there are spheres that do not bring such vain power struggles to bear. Transcendent ways of being can begin here, but eventually they move on to other realms, other planets, other stars."

I gazed up at the night sky. The Pleiades appeared from behind a small silvery cloud. "How does the Tree of Life grow all three of its levels?" I asked. "How does the Tree keep growing into the cosmos?"

He smiled gently. "First Creation begins with First Fire, the fire of illuminated awareness within the black void of space. From that First Fire comes the Spirit Water, the vapors. As the First Fire grows in its awareness, it fuses in a marriage with ecstatic aspects of itself and the void. These married aspects condense eventually after they merge together. They soothe and activate one another, forming something new—a nectar, an elixir, a vapor, the Spirit Water. First Fire and Spirit Water then refine and interact and we have Lightning Wisdom and Rainbow Essence. These are the elements of Paradise and they are eventually deposited as the growing Earth. As all of the elements coalesce, they bubble and form Earth matter. From Earth matter, water and fire and wood can grow—the sprouting shaft, and the Tree of Life on Earth. The ecstasy of the Tree of Life produces a sigh, the breath that is the air. That air becomes the Breath of Life for all beings on the Earth level. And from that Breath of Life, caressed by light and by the warmth of fire, cooled by the nectar of water and refined by the elements of Rainbow Essence, the Spirit that is evolving now in each of us begins to grow.

"This occurs if all circulates in a holistic way, as it is intended to do. Whenever any element becomes self-important and tries to consume more power for itself to expand its territory, you will have imbalance, suffering, conflict, struggle, delusion, attachment, and death. The evolving Spirit, if grown properly in the garden of life, can go on beyond the heavy elements of Earth in a refined body of Rainbow Essence, and it will inhabit the realms of the Fires of Illumination, the Waters of Spirit, and the Lightning of Wisdom, and will cross the Bridge of Rainbow Essence. It will inhabit the top portion of the Tree of Life where all the joy and freedom reside. This is pure new Earth.

"In one's life one must continually cook oneself like this succulent feast we are preparing here. One must be fragrant, aromatic—simply delicious. Each time a dish of our heavy elements is prepared, we call all the forces of creation for whom we wish to offer ourselves to come and partake of the feast. We offer our feast with compassion. All those at the table consume our dish and are nourished by it, since it is food for them. In the process of offering ourselves, we are strengthened and we release any aspect of our being that is clinging to the old heavy portions that are being consumed. Thus we transmute our attachments into an incorruptible generosity and gratitude. This yields us an inexhaustible source of free energy with which we continue to sustain the subtle essential refinement.

"After the heavy elements are eaten away, only a more refined essence remains, which is indigestible as a source of fuel. Only very evolved beings can truly understand such mysteries and offerings. Most beings are far too stingy, corruptible, childish, fearful, and exhaustible. However, the Universe itself empowers these offerings, because the purpose of all this is to continue to evolve, to soar, not to stay forever and cling. That is impossible anyway. All of this is utterly impermanent. Even the Earth herself, the Sun, the Moon, the Universe—all form is impermanent and it does not like that truth until it becomes very wise, sublime, and evolved."

I was speechless as I stared into the fire. Thank heaven the deer meat feast was ready. Later that night I decided to explore this wisdom further in Dreaming and I set myself a task to Dream my offering to the Tree of Life each and every night from that one forward. The process deepened during every instance of Dreaming until entire nights were devoted exclusively to preparation, Dreamed ceremony, and the offerings themselves. The culminating offering was Dreamed all in one night and once it was made, I understood that the entire offering sequence had been very pleasing.

The Dreaming began with two altar platforms standing in an empty Dreamscape. Between the two platforms an immense tree stood, with thick branches reaching up to the sky, softly rippling in a gentle breeze. I had three bodies. Each one was dressed in white and my awareness was simultaneously in each of them. On the first altar platform, I lay down on my back to be in touch with the base foundation level of being. I opened my own chest by simply reaching inside it, and I extracted and offered my heart to the sky shining brightly through the branches of the great tree. There was no pain and no blood flow. My heart dissolved into the sky and the offering was filled with ecstasy and relief.

On the second platform I stood erect, like a tree of the Earth. The breeze caressed my body and my white dress billowed. Beings of vapor and spirit came down from the sky, stood before the altar platform, and threw a crystal dagger into my heart. The front of my white dress turned red and damp as though someone had thrown a chalice of red wine at my breast. I had the sensation there of bursting grapes. My second body fell. The crystal dagger then became the open wings of a luminous bird and my heart became the body of the bird. It flew out of my chest and went up into the sky with the Sky Beings. They all dissolved in their upward flight like a rainbow fading as it ascends to the heights.

My third body was watching all that went on in the first two offerings. Then a huge butterfly appeared flying in the sky. It circled around and around the crown of my head. I could hear the soft vibration of its wings as it flew, making a halo formation around the top of my skull. The length of the butterfly's body stretched all the way from my inner eye down to the very base of my skull. The butterfly was so enormous that its wingspan encompassed both lobes of my brain. It landed on the crown of my head and spread its wings out fully over my skull, tickling my brain, and I awoke from the Dream.

When I opened my eyes to the world of everyday life, I received an irrefutable, unshakable certainty, a confirmation that the offering had been accepted. Don Juan was absolutely elated. I don't think I ever saw him so stimulated, so intrigued or excited at any other moment. Meanwhile, he also seemed to have a keen interest in testing my understanding of what had gone on.

"You realize that your perception is the pure untethered perception of Dream Power, don't you?" he asked me. "What I mean is that these moments we share, what we do and experience here, what we live and See, our intent, the way we communicate with one another, what we feel . . . it is something that we share and confirm for one another and agree upon because we both See and communicate and experience at these levels. A person without the language of Dream Power would be an outsider and would see and understand and receive little or none of it. They might see some of the power and even witness the truly miraculous, according to their understanding, but they wouldn't get all of it, and they would talk and reduce themselves out of much of what they did experience, instead of expanding their awareness and their actions. I can assure you of that. The energy is out of their grasp.

"If you ever wish to share any of this—and you will wish to do so, for who could deny sharing a little bit of this treasure with a world so desperate? If you ever do share some of it, you will have to select very well what you share. Be careful and deliberate. Just a tiny little bit—one grain will go a very long way."

I thought of the quote by William Blake: "See the world in a grain of sand . . ."

"You will have to learn to bridge the languages so that you may communicate the truth that needs to be shared in the language of Dream Power with integrity, in a manner that someone who speaks only the limited ordinary languages that they are taught in everyday life can understand. You may perhaps find yourself speaking in parables, or in stories, or with poetic flair so that you may say something truthful and profound, beyond the boundaries of limited concepts, in eloquent, simple words.

"This is one of the skills of the language of Dream Power and among the people here, this Dreaming verbal capacity is highly prized in the leaders who must speak for the many, guide, advise, interpret Dreams accurately, and convey medicine wisdom. Your throat, your tongue will have a potency, but more than that, ultimately, whatever you say will always be backed up by the energy of Dream Power. The pure truth will always appear, although it may not appear in the overly simplistic or the overcomplicated fashions of those who speak the languages of everyday life. This will bring up conflicts in them regarding their descriptions of what they call 'reality.' And this corroboration of your utterances will be astonishing at first, even to you.

"It is quite a valuable teaching tool and very essential when you serve as counsel. You may find yourself in the position of educating those with whom you share this counsel. You may even teach some rudimentary words and ways of assembling some of the concepts, a simple version of the language of Dream Power with which they may pray and leap to formulate thoughts about things for which they have no frame of reference, things they have never experienced and are told do not even exist, things they are told are impossible or even forbidden. You will develop artistry in this.

"In whatever manner you convey the language of Dream Power—be it through the skillful use of the words of everyday life, through medicine songs and prayers, with Dreaming itself, through other practices, offerings and ceremonies, energetic work, or even by calling the energetic presences or your own examples—it will be very good medicine. The energy will live within you more and more as you distill the intent into totally direct, utterly powerful sincerity.

"You could say that we experience what we experience, the possibilities and the unlimited access here in these realms, because this is where we live. You could also say that others have the experiences they do because they reside in other realms, in other realities. They do not live or even belong here. Yet there are some very useful things from here that can help them where they are, seeds that they can plant in their own soil. You might say that on Earth there are many planets and that we live on one while there are many others who live on another. The realities are as different and as distant as that, and yet there is a way to communicate between different planets and a way to share a few things of benefit between them."

"I see the truth of it," I replied. I was truly in awe of what I had seen and heard and of all the energy that was now in movement. I recalled a previous conversation that had occurred one evening with don Juan in which he had commented that one of the most basic universal languages of energy is that of the conveying of information through movement. I marveled at all the artificially contrived, arbitrary, utterly unnecessary, confining cultural structures of language that actually serve to confound humanity, its movement, and its perception, and buffer it from the utterly sublime elegant simplicity and the universal comprehension of the genuine and original, natural, innate language. A tower of Babel had crashed on the people of the world and in that moment they seemed as blind, outcast, and confused as I had ever perceived them.

I realized that even their conceptions of themselves were nothing but shabby structures formed from this delusion, and I wondered why it was so hard for them to dissolve it all back into the original awareness. I was so happy that I was in a world where such an intent was the simple and total pursuit. To realize the original nature from which all things come and to evolve in the possibilities present there without clinging or creating pain and suffering seemed somehow to be the only worthwhile time spent in life. Even time itself had shown its nature to be beyond description.

I decided then and there that after everything I had thus far seen and experienced, and considering all the suffering and the hardships that almost every sentient being experiences at one time or another, some for an entire lifetime, it could do absolutely no harm whatsoever to share some of the deeper understandings that I was receiving.

I realized that this would be like opening the world to a new possibility or pathway. As I Dreamed later that night I saw a vessel, something like a new Noah's ark made of rainbows and filled with awareness, sailing off into the infinite and sublime potential of the Celestial realms.

Practice Four

Making an Offering
of Ourselves

1. Perhaps the best and the simplest way to begin this process of transmutation is to go straight to the heart of the matter and offer our hearts. Begin each night's Dreaming with the simplest of intents, to Dream your heart, nothing more and nothing less.

2. As the Dreaming continues, you will discover what heart is and you will learn much and bring up many things about yourself that are exquisite, unfathomable, and wondrous and that need to be nurtured, freed, and allowed. You will also bring up the understanding of wounds and traumas, and uncharitable, insincere ways of being that have to be released.

3. Follow this process and as you continue to Dream your heart, ask your Dreaming: Can this be reconciled? Can this be healed? Can this be unified and fulfilled? What is the right process and where is the clear path that I should follow? How may I grow the treasures of heart? Is this something I might share? Where is the pure essence within? May I accept this? Is this something that needs to be allowed to go? If so, how may I release this? How may I be just, honorable, brave, and forgiving? How may I find the joy? Is this free, strong, and loyal?

4. Set your intent each night before you enter into Dreaming and follow the language of your Dreams, as though you

were listening to one chapter of a bedtime story every night. Find comfort and solace in the one who is recounting your Dreaming.

5. Awaken several times during the night to reset your intent and to review what you have Dreamed thus far. This is a very good practice. If taking notes is helpful to you, you may do so.

6. When you go into and return into Dreaming, make of yourself a living offering. Be still in your bed in a position of offering with your arms stretched to the sides at heart level, or relax with your hands crossed over your heart. Intend to Dream from the heart, listen to your heart, and offer your heart for further opening.

7. To find your heart, press the center of your chest until you encounter a feeling of warmth and well-being. When you do, you've found it.

5

Beyond the Mother Earth

It was time to face the dark Anti-Mother. Doña Celestina was sitting out under her ramada late in the afternoon wearing a long black skirt and rocking slightly in a bent wooden rocking chair, tapping her left foot softly on the adobe porch floor. The autumn desert was beginning to cool down and there was a slight breeze.

"Did you have a good time?" she asked, calling out from the rocker as I walked toward the front porch. Her inflection made the question sound as though it were a parody of a mother interrogating a wayward teenager returning home late from a date.

"Yes, ma'am," I replied politely as my mother had always insisted I do when speaking with women elders. I stepped onto the porch with my downcast eyes focused on every grain of sand on the path and every pore in the adobe floor. Doña Celestina was more than a woman elder, I thought; she was a completely new archetype, as was don Juan.

"And so are you," doña Celestina said to me, clearly reading my thoughts as I surveyed her in amazement. I cringed. "You are new," she reiterated with emphasis.

Doña Celestina invited me to a glass of cool mineral water and I sat down with her on the porch in the other bent wooden rocker. "Now you are ready to accompany me in my work and learn," she stated firmly.

I gulped as I swallowed the fresh sparkling water.

"Now you can see what respect really is," she said cryptically. "More than that, you are going to start the work now that I have set out for you. Some clients are coming here tonight from the Bacatete Sierra for an energetic exorcism. You are going to help me in the preparations and in the process and witness everything that goes on. This may not be something that is needed in the realms of Celestial spirit, but it is definitely something that is required from time to time on Earth and in the Underworld."

I took stock of all my experiences since I had left her backyard in the early morning over a month ago with Carlo Castano. What she was referring to regarding my preparedness was evident. I had changed, and my view of life, the world, and what is possible had changed along with it. I was a new being, empty and ready to accept a new, cleansed world.

As night fell, we began to set up a mesa in the altar room for the *mitote*, an all-night seance or ceremony of communion. We emptied the entire room completely except for the large wooden table and quite a few wooden chairs. We placed candles at the four corners of the room and an altar cloth upon the table. The problem, doña Celestina informed me as we swept and dusted the space, was an epidemic of tuberculosis in the Bacatete mountain range and in the Copper Canyon. It was running rampant and affecting many of the Pima and the Tarahumara Indians, who did not all have continued access to or complete confidence in Western drugs and had requested a ceremony.

The preparations were very straightforward. I was to keep the door to the altar room wide open and allow the wind to flow into the space. I was to tend the fire outside at the fire pit in the back quadrangle of the property and keep it burning all night with the embers red-hot. I was then to carry embers from the fire pit in an earthen coal scuttle and stoke a brazier with the red-hot embers. I had a small ceramic pot filled with yellow sulfur powder, mineral salts, eucalyptus resin, and myrrh. I was to drop the powder in minute quantities onto the hot embers on top of the brazier and keep this burning all during the exorcism. The essences would expose, heal, thwart, and cook the energies attached to the epidemic of tuberculosis, doña Celestina assured me. There was also an offering bowl placed on the mesa for the antitubercular drugs. I was to collect samples of these from the villagers and they too would be cleansed, empowered, and blessed during the night's energetic work.

The villagers from the Sierra arrived at about nine in the evening carrying a large medicine bundle, a cloth filled with items from all of the affected areas that was tied in a knot at the top. The sacred items in the bundle had all been blessed by the local shamans before the collective medicine was placed into the large cloth and this was to stand in for the populations of all the petitioning villages and for those villagers who were too ill to travel.

The bundle was placed on the mesa, which was covered with a blue-black altar cloth. I set the brazier directly under the mesa. The villagers from the Sierra seated themselves in the straight-backed wooden chairs all around the altar and doña Celestina informed them that I was going to assist her in the work. She explained to them that I was learning how to do what she did. They all looked at me with respect and nodded.

Doña Celestina then left the altar room and undid her head-rag turban. It was the first time I had ever seen her black, gray, and white hair worn completely loose. Her straight mass of long coarse hair hung wildly down past her elbows. She brought her huge machete in with her when she returned to the room and placed it sternly upon the mesa. She then signaled for me to begin offering the powdered essences.

The fumes and vapors and smoke quickly wafted and filled

the room with the smells of hot rotten eggs, menthol, salt, and sweet earth, and a thick fog began to hang in the air like an other-worldly entity. Almost as soon as the smoke reached the open doorway, all sizes and colors of desert scorpions began to crackle and crunch and like a little army they started to march in from outside, making their way across the sands in the back quadrangle. They came from who-knows-what tiny little holes into the room and crawled all around the floor and eventually even onto the mesa itself.

Doña Celestina told me discreetly that if they came very near me but none of them crawled on me, and especially if none of them stung me, it would be a very good sign for my future work. She said they were attracted by the sulfur and that they were the guardians of the ceremony. Somehow I knew that if I conveyed fearless, harmonious, respectful energy to the scorpions, they would respect me, too, and I would remain unstung. This was the case all during the night, although they came as close to me as I could comfortably tolerate, prancing around right before my eyes, strutting in the smoke with their stingers up.

I was not ready for what happened next. Doña Celestina picked up the machete like a hatchet woman and her eyes rolled back deeply into their large sockets. She began to spin and swing the machete with a lethal precision and she uttered a guttural rhythmic chant as she did so. She reeled around the room thrusting the machete and hacking at the air. She gyrated on one foot and twirled as the machete sang its strokes. It went on and on and on. I stoked the fire and the brazier endlessly.

All of the villagers seated in the chairs and I myself in time began to see greenish entities or energies in the smoke. Doña Celestina was actually dismembering and decapitating those spirits, or perhaps they were the internal demons that were consuming the spirits of all the ill persons in the affected villages. Occasionally, someone had to leave the room and wretch. The spinning sensation caused by her movements and by those of the machete, combined with the glint of steel, the fervent chanting, and the acrid blanket of fumes, heat, and vapors, was totally dizzying.

As the night wore on, the villagers began to nod, sleep, and Dream in their chairs. At one moment in the dead of night, brought on by the trance of all the focused exertion and the nonordinary reality of the ceremony, I experienced a bilocation. One part of me was stoking the brazier and another part was simultaneously tending the fire at the fire pit. In the altar room I was watching doña Celestina gyrate on one leg, circling the villagers and swinging a spinning machete, and at the fire, I was at the same time watching her roast and consume pieces of all the spirits she had hacked into bits. She was consuming the consumers and the possessors. Her acts and her level of awareness seemed to completely nullify or transmute their existence. The deep trance she maintained gave her an irrefutable understanding. I began to see long shadows, or fang-style tattoos and war paint, that appeared periodically on her chin, or perhaps it was even dripping blood showing up in the glow of the firelight.

Suddenly the fire in the fire pit started to leap and swell and roar as though it had been doused with oil or alcohol. All of the villagers began to stir in their chairs and I came back to my sense of one location. The candles were about half of the way burned down at the four corners of the altar room and their flames started to flicker and dance with an imperceptible wind. Doña Celestina instructed me to untie the medicine bundle on the altar and let that wind blow through all of the sacred items that had been brought in from the villages. Then she actually chased the wind around the altar room with her machete. I have never seen a being move with such speed in my entire life. I could genuinely perceive the trails left in the air from her movements.

The energetic dross seemed to fall as though it was

disconnected from the air and all was absorbed back into the earth. The energy of the epidemic had been subdued. In time, I tied the bundle up again as she instructed and the fire started to go out. It was a very good sign. Doña Celestina remarked that it should now be allowed to burn down to ash, for dawn was coming and everyone would Dream for a while.

I followed her instructions and went straight to my room. I was so deep into the energy that I felt like a somnambulist. Falling onto the bed facedown with all of my clothes on, I went directly into Dreaming. Suddenly I was riding on the back of a huge flying dragon of rainbow colors. It was a giant wind dragon that was flowing like an air current through the vast opening of a deep canyon in Tibet. All of the monks, dressed in red and gold and orange robes, came running out of a monastery with long trumpets and longer horns, which they perched at the very edge of the precipice. They began to sound these horns loudly and deeply into the chasm. The abyss vibrated. The rows of monks at the canyon's edge resounded the horns and cheered as the dragon and I flew by. The dragon had allowed itself to be ridden and I rode in triumph and joy. I waved at them like a little girl as we whisked past.

Then I was an adult communing with other Tibetan males at an outdoor stand decorated with fluttering multicolored prayer flags that was offering children's books. At first I was a male myself, but then I transformed from a Tibetan man into a mixture of a Caucasian and a Tibetan woman with long braids. We were in the high snowy mountains, at the roof of the world, making an offering to the people. I was throat singing and multitonal chanting with the males and all the local people were attracted by the chants.

A fat woman with a baby waddled up to the stand to buy a book for her child. The Tibetans were debating about whether I had truly been singing like a monk, as a woman. One Tibetan who was standing in the very middle of the group said, "I witnessed the transformation myself. She was throat singing, although you could not understand the words."

The woman with the child tapped her foot impatiently, waiting to be paid attention to so that she could buy a book. She praised the content of the books and remarked how lovely they were and how good they would be for her child. One of the monks kindly said to her, "I am not interested in such an unimpressive love." This customer became very irate, angry, and envious. She wanted to compete with me for my transformation.

She stomped off to her village, found a huge rubber ball, came back with it, and threw it at my abdomen, hoping that some of my transformation would splash back on her as though I were made of water. I picked up the ball and hurled it at her. She either had to drop the baby or give up the ball. She chose to hold on to the baby and thus lost it, ultimately, and lost the game that she had started. All of the transformation that she had coveted came back to me. She became even fatter and very nearsighted, and all of her beautiful clothes turned to those of a milkmaid. She thumped and jiggled away with an awareness of what she was and of what she had done.

I opened my eyes to another level of awareness. It was daylight and Carlo Castano was peeking his head into my bedroom window. The villagers had long since left with their bundle, heading back to the Sierra after a successful ceremony. Doña Celestina was in seclusion; she was not available and she would not be for days. She was deep into the work and meditation after the ceremony as she had energetic tasks of closure to perform.

Carlo was heading off to Mexico City. He was going to see a Tibetan medical doctor who was visiting there with a group of monks, and he had stopped by because he wanted to know if I'd like to come along. He hinted that there might be the possibility of talking with some of the visiting lamas regarding the

Dreaming practices of Tibet and their similarities to the Dreaming practiced by Mesoamerican shamans.

My Dreaming had foretold this and I found myself dragging my body into his car half asleep, without breakfast, without changing clothes, and without questions. It just seemed logical and I needed a big change after that ceremony. I was done in. Carlo said there was no need for me to bring anything. He had plenty of money and he'd pay for the whole trip. Doña Celestina was already aware of his invitation. He had seen her in the morning as she was sweeping up some of the ash from the fire.

So I quietly went along and I slept in the front seat half of the way to Mexico City. We arrived there the next morning. Carlo had managed to drive all throughout the day and night without exhaustion, and he calmly and effortlessly navigated the national capital, a colossus of over 35 million inhabitants, and the monstrous downtown traffic. He was a real city dweller. We checked into two rooms at the Hotel Montejo in the Zona Rosa, the theater zone, and slept until late that afternoon. After showering, we took a walk through the tree-lined Alameda Park and then headed to one of Mexico City's many fine Chinese restaurants for an early dinner. It was our first meal since we had been on the road and we were famished.

The rapid change in ambiance from a ceremony in the outback of Sonora to an evening dinner in the federal district was absolutely astonishing. I sat in a daze as I gazed upon the elegant red-and-gold decor of the small alcove where we were seated. For Carlo, it seemed to be nothing drastic. He graciously ordered oolong tea, cold barbecued pork with hot mustard, and Mongolian beef. I requested chrysanthemum tea, egg drop soup, and a dish called dragon and phoenix, made with diced lobster and breast of chicken. He settled back into his chair in the reddish golden room filled with lantern light.

"I am in my element in a place like this," he remarked, satisfied. "It's not the people that I seek, although one happens upon marvels now and then. It's the inorganic labyrinth that I like. You don't like the city much, do you?"

I pondered his opening thoughts. "Oh, I don't mind it when there is art on display or theater, and good food." I laughed. "I love beautifully designed public strolling spaces, gardens and parks, fountains . . . and I appreciate the fine architecture and public sculpture. I like clean cities with good weather that are a mixture of the ancient and the modern, well blended. I'm interested in a city's crowning collective aspirations, in the artist colonies and in the multicultural public markets. In Mexico City, I love all of the murals here, the artist colonies, the parks, and also the Museum of Anthropology. I like to visit the university campuses in cities I go to, if they are notable, and I also go to the libraries. But you're right, I'm more of a small-town or village dweller. I enjoy being able to see the edge of the place where I live and experience only nature beyond it. I like peace. I'll bet you even like the subways, don't you?"

Carlo raised his brow at my answer. There was a mischievous glimmer in his eyes. "I don't come from a place like this," he said, "but I have gotten used to it and it's very stimulating for the mind. I'm probably much more quiet than you think. When I'm in public I can become very animated, but I also have my reclusive side. I can be out and about with a nonhuman focus and I also enjoy going very deeply. Like you, I've done my share of travel and investigation in my life, but that's not all that I am."

I was quite aware that Carlo Castano was more than a traveler. He had met many notable individuals in his field of endeavors and his ideas were taken seriously by some great artists and thinkers. Still, I was able to see that his public persona was like a very fine suit that he sincerely deserved, but that it was not his favorite suit in the closet and was one that he wore infrequently. I was thankful of that, and very interested to find out more about the rest of him and what he was, and I sensed that might come.

The waiter brought us our main courses. We ate in enthusiastic silence. It was obvious that we were both quite hungry and enjoyed a good meal. The food was also delicious. Surprisingly, Mexico City has some of the world's best Chinese restaurants, outside of China, due to its large immigrant population and a liberal trade relationship. After our meal Carlo ordered dried lychee fruits for our desert. It was the first time I had ever tried them and they were exquisite, quite potent, chewy, smoky sweet, and succulent.

We walked back to the hotel, passing through as many local parks as we could on the way. He had a shuffling stroll that I enjoyed observing out of the corner of my eye. "I like the way you Dream," he finally said, smiling up at me. "All of this is very visionary. Everything we experience together has an audacious artistic flair and vibrancy. You are continually in a trance. There's a field of joy and true Seeing all around us and it's very provocative. I perceive an elegance that I can't quite compare to anything else. Every moment seems to bubble with life and nothing is taken for granted as being too real. It's as though you Dream the whole town, right around us."

I smirked, covering my mouth with my hand, and gazed at the panoramas we were passing through. They were temporal and circuslike, impressionistic experiences, as though they were created of ethereal oil on living canvas, painted by a master invisible artist behind the scenes with whom I had an intimate, sanctioned, and secret relationship. One bubble of perception stretched until we entered another. Everyone seemed festive somehow. I had been given the keys to every mystery. My ally was a universal toy maker who could demonstrate the delight of all reality, that it can be rather like a set of little Russian dolls, with one cheerful, unexpected, unfathomable essence peeking out from within another. I could have walked all night.

I watched the particular dancelike swing of Carlo's footsteps. "I like your Dreaming, too," I finally commented. "You allow this. You are most intelligent yet you can yield and be truly, deeply silent. You work hard and are capable and relentless and elegant in your intent, even if your perceptions go a long way off, even if you disappear into the vastness. I sense skillful multilevel architectural design in your Dreaming, and an abstract structure that I am beginning to find quite sublime. There's something even deeper that I like even more. You remain empty and aware, and something that is profoundly nonordinary doesn't totally scare you off. Now if we could just synchronize or harmonize, I think we could have quite a journey into uncharted territory."

He laughed. We shuffled along afterward in silence and arrived at the hotel door. Carlo walked me to my room and bowed before I entered. I smiled and returned the bow. His room was right across the hall. My sleep wasn't usual that night. I slept and yet I was awake throughout the night, if one can experience such a thing. My body seemed to rush with energy, and although I was tired, I had more energy than I was accustomed to having, which seemed to be replenishing me at a vibratory level. When I finally slept as I am accustomed to sleeping, it was only for a few hours, and then a little after dawn I was wide awake and felt wonderful.

The next afternoon I went with him to his appointment. I sat in the living room of a quaint Mexican home in one of the city's more pleasant and airy suburbs while Carlo consulted with the visiting Tibetan medical doctor in another room. The Tibetans had become quite interesting to me of late. I had discovered that their culture had once been very warlike, similar to the Apache, quite ruthless and fearless. Then at a given moment in their history they had made the collective decision to adopt Buddhist philosophy into their shamanic tradition and to practice strict nonviolence without any conquering influence from the outside. That was a most impressive transformation, to my way of thinking.

During the time I was waiting in the living room, a lama dressed in red and orange robes walked in. I gathered that Tibetan monks were coming to Mexico City on a semiregular basis and that they were setting up a center and offering many ceremonies, in response to invitations. The lama sat down near me and handed me a book from one of the shelves about *dakinis*, enlightened female beings, and another book about a female Tibetan mystic by the name of Machig Labdron. He looked at me, smiled sweetly, and said, "much wisdom." Then he indicated with signs that I should begin to read while I sat waiting.

I read the little book about Machig Labdron while Carlo was in consultation. I selected this one because feminine ecstasy and mysticism was my favorite area in the study of global spirituality. The ordinary female is still often quite repressed within religions and within spiritual disciplines, but the ecstatic or mystical female is a hands-off kind of affair. The tradition will stand back, remove the glass ceiling, and let her be holy. It will allow the female to have this sacred experience, if it is genuine, and it is greatly revered.

The book was written in a style called sacred biography and it detailed a religious saint and her spiritual development. The account included many of her miraculous attainments, expressed with the understanding that such transcendence is possible and does in fact happen. She had first emanated from a female deity. She had incarnated as a male mystic who attained incorruptibility meditating in a cave, and then she transferred her energy body into the body of a female child so that enlightenment could be achieved in a woman's body. She even left her own child with relatives at the tender age of four so that she could become illuminated for all women and bring teachings to Tibet.

The book offered brief explanations of the means and methods of her transformations and of some of the practices and teachings that she had received in her life, and also of those that she had developed herself while in Dreaming and in meditation, which she later taught to her lineage. One of the practices was called Chöd, and it was remarkably like the exorcism that doña Celestina had performed, with some minor variations. The book indicated that practitioners of Chöd, called *chödpas,* were called during epidemics in Tibet, and that they also hacked up the corpses in the cemeteries for sky burial, an offering of the dead body to the vultures. They were called in because as a result of the practice, chödpas became totally immune to contamination.

I was astounded at the similarities in practice and at the bridge that my Dreaming had built for me. The lama came into the room again and touched the area between his eyebrows with his second finger. He nodded toward my forehead. "Much wisdom," he said again, and he laughed like a child.

I smiled at him and laughed back.

"The practices you do now, you keep doing these," he said and laughed once more.

I grinned and blushed a little bit.

"Wisdom is female, in the blood," he said.

I sat in silence.

Carlo returned to the living room after his medical consultation. He seemed light and vigorous. He sat down in a stuffed armchair and told me that the visiting monks were making an offering of a sand painting in one of the buildings at the National University. The monk who had lent me the books waved at us and indicated that we should go to see it. Carlo and I both felt that this was a good idea. When we arrived on the

campus and found the right place, the mandala sand painting
was just being finished. We managed to see this representation
of a sacred universe before the monks who had created it
offered a ceremony of closing and swept all of the rainbow-
colored sands back into their deconfigured state. They blew
long horns during the closing ceremony and although it was a
teaching regarding the impermanence and emptiness of form, it
was very joyful. The mandala had been dedicated to a deity
called The Terrifier of Death and to the path of enlightenment
in one lifetime.

The next morning Carlo and I began to drive gradually back to
Sonora. He had an appointment to keep in California, he con-
fided. When I arrived at doña Celestina's home on the following
day, she had already decided on a new course of instruction for
me. Doña Celestina didn't believe in explaining the work. You
just did it and that was all. One learned from experience and
that meant avoiding too many descriptions that might be imitated in exchange for true understanding. Thus upon returning
to her home, she said nothing about what had gone on in the
exorcism ceremony. It was self-evident. She said nothing about
Carlo and nothing about the monks. Instead, she had a task for
me to perform. When I told her about the Chöd practice, she listened profoundly, but without comment.

Doña Celestina was a taskmaster regarding self-importance.
She could send you into the basement of your being for it. She
simply would not tolerate an ounce of self-worship or indulgence. That meant you worked your way up to attain understanding and mastery at every level and you faced all your
pettiness. Mastery required Seeing and courage. There was no
place for stubbornness or social sucking up. She could seem
wrathful in her intent upon excellence and she exacted a generosity of effort or there was no deal; and she reciprocated with

all of her intensity and energy. If contemplation was the order of the day, you were to spend all day and night on that and nothing else. You could find all the truth and beauty genuinely present in the practice, work, or offering, but you stayed focused, and you never let your lesser desires divert you.

The doña didn't pamper anyone and she could not be approached with insincerity. She could be forceful, almost to the point of brutality. Yet she had a sense of one's innate strengths and never forced a person to take the wrong direction, that is, if you were obedient. She would force you to take the right direction, though. Disobedience was not an option. It constituted total eviction. One was utterly cast out and with a heavy energetic weight to bear. Yet one was free to disobey, if one understood the totally undesirable consequences and could survive them to learn.

For doña Celestina, wantonness was one of the female's worst qualities, accompanied by frivolity, envy, vanity, greed, ignorance, and dishonesty. She would not tolerate theft or lies or cowardice, even in the most destitute women she taught. She'd send them packing without understanding. The repercussions of our individual and collective acts and the absolute truth are more than terrifying enough, and their weight was as heavy a load as she would put up with in any apprentice. There were other ways to show your spirit besides the disobedience of direct energetic wisdom.

She admired strength and artistry, and she insisted that we come to understand and face up to the truths about ourselves, whatever those truths might be—absolute and relative, sublime, infinite, horrendous, infantile, bizarre, or otherwise. In that light, we had endless discussions about the plight of women after my return from Mexico City. However, a conversation with an archetypal being like doña Celestina was not an ordinary conversation. She would say something simple and powerful from the depths and then convey encyclopedic volumes with her mind, her intent, her gaze, her Dreaming, and her example. Thus I "heard" much more than she actually "spoke," and this was precisely as she intended. That is the only way to comprehend it.

"The whole issue of reproduction is a difficult topic for women," doña Celestina said one night, opening a new theme as we worked making candles in the altar room. "Ideally birth should occur at a replacement level, if that. Only those with missions in life are necessary to the whole of life. Many humans are just necessary to themselves nowadays. They take on a false identity or a false mission as a means to justify themselves." She held up a fresh golden taper and twirled it by the wick.

I grimaced at her way of saying things.

"Just think of it this way: think of the extra resources that would be available, more food, more doctors for each patient, and more teachers for each student, less pollution, less exploitation of nature, and less conflicts."

"That's true," I agreed. I sat back for a moment to think. I watched two large moths fly into the room through the open doorway and then repeatedly circle the pot of molten golden wax. One moth lighted on the pile of wicks.

"Women don't need to be validated by someone else and many can take care of themselves better than they are cared for by others," she went on, bent on her topic as she lifted another taper out of the wax. "There are alternative ways of caring for one another and they should be explored. All different kinds of families can exist; we don't need to make too many people just to show that we have one! Perhaps losing someone obligates us to find that being has changed form, or lost form. Or perhaps it sends us on a quest to receive the next ones who will come to us for that being, as a tree comes from the seed, to bring us many messages like the birds in its branches, until we too depart."

I thought of loved ones who had departed their previous form, and I slipped into reverie, gazing in the darkness and the candlelight.

"I don't usually speak gently, but I will for a moment, and I'll also be frank," she continued. "When a woman becomes a mother, her upward growth is at a standstill for quite a time and many do not develop the wisdom or the compassion to compensate for that. So they compete. Motherhood should only be a necessary thing, not a casual one. In fact, women do not want to realize that conception breaks the ascending male nature in both partners. Conceiving too often puts unnecessary weight on life. Even the children can't catch up. It's too consumptive. Infinite diversity in existence occurs gradually, or even instantaneously, but not just as the result of an explosion in reproduction.

"The feminine aspect can cling to a cyclical way of being, and if that way of being includes too many children, it will carve up too much for food, in the same way that both the male and female aspects have the tendency to carve up too much for knowledge. This creates a vicious machine. It is not optimal and it will ultimately dissatisfy the male aspect. Both are injured by the excessive carving. Remember, we must find the possibility of a dynamic marriage between them. If the male aspect is dissatisfied, it will depart for cosmic territory and it will not bless. It will eventually lose interest in and dissatisfy the female. It may even abandon her. It may become angry. Then the female aspect becomes angry or sad and clings even more to her own nature or to the children to satisfy the needs that are not met by her male counterpart. What you have there is a split, a conflict between cyclical nature and upright nature, between the volcano fire of the feminine and the glacial spirit of the male."

"What will satisfy it?" I asked her, truly intrigued.

"That's where the machete comes in." She smiled slyly and her teeth glinted in the flickering candlelight. "No more being gentle. Sooner or later both of them, even the feminine, has got to let go and say good-bye to Mother. It is not quite our totality. And knowledge is a crutch that has to be dropped, too. Then masculine and feminine might truly find each other. There are some women in traditional cultures who serve as priestesses for an entire lifetime, totally devoted to the Mother Earth and to the Sacred Feminine of the Earth. There are celibate sisterhoods. There are also priesthoods, celibate brotherhoods, and then the common marriages in these current circumstances. Even so, most don't develop beyond this. There are more possibilities out there, and adventures. We can truly grow upward, for what mother wishes only that role of motherhood forever? What child wishes ultimately only to grow to be a parent forever? We can embody something else. There is such a thing as an energetic consort.

"Human beings do not always need to succumb to reproductive urges. Sexuality and reproduction are in fact very different. Only ignorance tells the human race that the two are the same thing. In holistic nature, reproduction is often but not always governed by the survival urge and wisdom of a species and that keeps everything in a sacred balance, until it's time for a change. The time for change comes whether we like it or not. A species will arrive at the point of an evolutionary departure. A new kind of vessel is being suggested. The lineage may be ready to move on, to journey, to develop further. So what must they do?"

"Someone becomes realized, luminous, enlightened," I interjected, casting my eyes toward the candle flame.

"Exactly," she replied. "Or they all do or die. We have to be willing to let go of the residue. Just as there is such a thing as being left behind, there is such a thing as being a guide. There are both degeneration and extinction, and there is also cooperation and evolution. Eventually this all has to go. It will all transmute. Even the Earth will transcend. What we need to do here is clean up."

I was silent in thought.

"Before you depart this Earth, there is only one thing remaining that I will ask of you first, one final task. You will transcend and I ask that before you go, you find strong women with powerful natures like your own and guide them in the right direction. You may even guide men. That is all. After that, you owe nothing and I will see to it that no toll is charged you at the gate."

"Thank you!" I said in tears, overwhelmed and truly moved.

"If I make a promise like that, I will keep it come what may, regardless of the form or lack of it that my energy may have at the time."

I had hit pure bedrock. I never felt such a certainty regarding anything in my life. That was not a human voice I had heard, but the voice of Mother Earth herself and of the Sacred Void Grandmother promising me that I would have a cosmic honeymoon and a sublime definitive journey.

Practice Five

The Boost of Mother Earth

1. This will only come with the Mother Earth's permission and cooperation. Here is how you begin. Go to a sacred place where the Mother Earth energy is very powerful and holistic. First ask permission to be there and then make an offering on the bare ground of pure water, milk, honey, seeds, and flowers. Ignite some coals and offer copal in a clay urn. Arrange everything like a mandala—a sacred circle on the ground—and place the burning copal in the center. Pour your heart out in prayer and express every meaningful intent that you have in your life. See the mandala offering like a portal through which you may speak to all the energies of the Earth while the copal billows. Thank all the energies of creation for your life and for your awareness and call them to listen.

2. Ask for guidance regarding what you need to do, what the tasks are that must be accomplished. Ask for revelations regarding debts that are owed by you which have to be repaid somehow in order to have the permission to live happily and freely, without illness, strife, and destruction. Request instructions on how to repay those debts.

3. Confess yourself and all of your failings and lack of awareness. Tell the Mother Earth exactly how you have felt in your life and how you wish to feel.

4. Ask for a good passing through life and death, for a good life itself, for love in your heart, and for the possibility to

find a good place at death. Ask for her help, guidance, and protection regarding your gradual transcendent illumination and liberation. Request that clear seeing be empowered by the overflowing love that she blesses you with in your heart.

5. Go and meditate. Find a tranquil place and sit and meditate for a time in silence. Now lie down with your head facing the east and Dream. Request for her voice and guidance to come to you in Dreaming and in the signs of nature. When you rise, regardless of what you have or have not yet received, express your gratitude. Have faith in and thankfulness for what you did receive and experience, and do not be envious of what you did not. Have confidence, even if what you received is currently imperceptible to you.

6. Before you depart the place, distribute the mandala offerings that have not been absorbed into the earth to the four directions. Request that the messages from the Mother Earth not abandon you and that they continue to come to you in Dreaming and be empowered and proven true in your waking world. Offer to return to that place, or to go to another sacred place with permission, and to continue to make offerings to keep the lines of communication open.

7. Understand that if she makes promises to you, and reveals wisdom to you, you are energetically and honor bound, and must do everything that she asks of you or you will never be free. Also understand that she will protect you as long as you honor her requests and fulfill them faithfully, and that when you have completed all that she asks of you, she will keep her promise and release you into a good place.

6

Exquisite Equilibrium

Carlo Castano came to visit us again one month later. Frankly, I was amazed that doña Celestina tolerated these continual interruptions from him. He was behaving like a suitor, not that I minded it. Rather, doña Celestina seemed to feel that the visits were designed by energy, that they were auspicious, and she admonished me to be kind and patient and to consider the fact that Carlo was offering me valuable options and opportunities that I might accept. There was an energetic liaison in the works.

On this occasion Carlo was driving all the way down to southern Mexico to the region of Oaxaca to visit several acquaintances, and on the return trip he was intending to stop in Mexico City again for a second appointment with the Tibetan physician. He casually announced that he was inviting to take me along on the whole journey and he was making a special effort to include an out-of-the-way excursion for me to meet with the Mazatec mushroom shaman Maria Sabina who lived in the tiny and remote Oaxacan mountain village of Huautla de Jimenez. Carlo said that this would most likely be my only opportunity to go so far back into those mountains and make her acquaintance.

Meanwhile doña Celestina simply insisted that I go visit with this woman shaman before she passed on and all of her wisdom was lost. War was erupting in Guatemala again and spilling over into the indigenous regions of the Mexican state of Chiapas, not far from Oaxaca. I expressed my legitimate concerns about traveling near a war zone, but Carlo assured me that we would be far back in the ancient mountains, away from civilization and from international borders, untouched, and that we would most likely not encounter any armed conflict.

Both of them seemed absolutely intent that I meet with all the genuine indigenous women of power that I had the possibility to encounter, especially elders, the likes of whom would never come again. It was part of the preparation for my task, doña Celestina reminded me. They each simply demanded that I go. So without voicing any more concerns, I packed several weeks' worth of clothes and piled them into Carlo's trunk, and we drove due south into more utterly unknown territory for me.

We traveled close to the Pacific coast whenever we could. Carlo remarked on the way that he loved the beauty of the beach and the sunny coastlines. I couldn't have agreed more. The drive to Oaxaca was going to be very long, he said. It would take us several days to get there, including all the rest stops. He would set a pleasant pace for the trip, but we would be driving continually. So I settled in, relaxed, and adjusted myself to the new idea.

I rode the first day in silence and contemplation. What strange fate was this? What forces in my life were propelling me in these directions? Is there such a thing as destiny? We stopped that first evening in the beach town of Guaymas and partook of a leisurely dinner together on a rustic oceanside patio. We began our feast with an appetizer of *ceviche*—a wide variety of the freshest diced raw seafood, prepared with lime juice, chopped tomato, raw jalapeno peppers, and onion. This sumptuous chilled salad was followed by a basket of hot corn tortillas, glasses of cool sparkling mineral water with lime, and two piping hot bowls of *sopa de mariscos,* an abundant and spicy seafood stew bathed in steaming red chili broth, containing all of the fresh fare of the local waters, plus boiled diced carrots and potatoes.

We calmly ate as we quietly watched the sun set over the desert coastline and shimmering ocean. We fortified ourselves for the days of our long drive ahead, receiving the energy of the breezes, the changing light, and all the potent beauty of the Baja gulf's bounty. After dinner, we took a walk along the beach together at dusk. The Baja tides can recede exceedingly far and the tide was out, so it was a beautiful stroll among the shell-laden sands.

We stopped for the night in the small town of Navajoa in the southwestern plains at the base of the Bacatete Sierra, the last substantial town before leaving the desert state of Sonora. Our drive had been peaceful after leaving the beach and we decided to avail ourselves of the only worthy place to rest. We slept soundly in a charming little hotel, spending some time sitting out in the garden courtyard before we went to our beds, and we started out fresh again in the morning. We drove all of the following day and spent the next night in the lush and temperate state of Nayarit. I read poetry aloud to Carlo for most of that day's trip. The scenery changed so frequently along our way that it seemed as though we passed through myriad microworlds, all connected by the Pan-American highway.

The next day, still heading south, we were ready for the trek yet farther onward to the state of Oaxaca. The villages were becoming quaint and picturesque as we progressed steadily. We were leaving man-made time behind and entering into humble fertile hills and valleys that seemed unchanged by the centuries or the pace of the Western world. I thought of the solace inherent in that kind of small village life out in nature and of how so much of the world is aching for it.

The road turned very mountainous when we entered the

state of Oaxaca the following afternoon. The range we were approaching dominated the horizon like the humped spine of an ancient, slumbering, giant dragon who dreamt on the land and sighed cloud puffs into the sky. We drove into the Sierra Madre del Sur mountain range and onto a narrow dirt road, which headed straight up to the top of the peaks. We jostled over them and went far back into that range, going around and around the endless mountains, up and over them and back down, up again and down again, spiraling and hanging over the edge at angles, bumping and jouncing.

I tend to turn greenish and get carsick in the mountains if I am not the driver and I kept asking, even pleading with Carlo to slow down. As it was, we proceeded at almost a crawl and my vertigo was nearly insurmountable. The sheer drops were quite daunting and there seemed to be no way out. Finally, when we were scarcely creeping, Carlo jokingly turned to me and asked if I would like for us to leave the car behind and hike the rest of the way. I almost considered it but we were much too far from the nearest village. Twilight was coming on and we were still circling the dizzying peaks deep in the center of the range. As we approached a fog bank at dark, we decided that we would have to spend the night parked on the side of the road and sleep in the front and backseats of the vehicle.

The night passed like the dream of approaching and receding mist. The abandoned roadside disappeared into the sheer awesomeness of primeval mountains and hanging cloud banks. We were swallowed by the dark central emptiness of the mountain range and its *axis mundi*. At dawn the next morning we roused ourselves, freshened with water we were carrying, and continued the slow trek through the mountains. The day was glorious and by noon we had finally arrived in Huautla.

The village was perched right at the summit and overlooked the flight of condors through a canyon. Most of the dwellings were wattle and daub with an occasional cement two-story whose second-floor windows opened onto the abyss. The focal point of the village was a large stone slab hewn right out of the mountaintop, which served as the marketplace, evoking the pre-Columbian markets of the fifteenth century. There a few humble Mazatec women were seated on *petates*—hand-woven straw mats—selling their potatoes and cilantro when we crossed the market plaza.

Maria Sabina's hut was at the outer edge of the village. We were led there by a local child along a winding steep trail. Doña Maria's middle-aged daughter greeted us when we arrived and led us into a small altar hut adjoining the residential hut. About five minutes later an elderly Mazatec Indian woman unceremoniously entered with curiosity. She was dressed in a clean white and red, elaborately patterned, hand-woven *huipil*, a traditional tunic of the area, and she appeared to be in her early eighties. She was highly alert, spritelike, and agile, with a delightful twinkle in her eyes. Her silvery white hair was freshly braided and she was as cheerful and radiant as the perfect mixture of a little girl and an unconventional old wise woman. She walked, or almost bounced and hopped, barefoot, and she was quite tiny. She only came up to my chest when we stood respectfully to greet her, standing a little shorter than Carlo.

Maria Sabina looked up at us and smiled. She had a bright, friendly, elder pixie countenance and good teeth for a woman living so far away from civilization. She gazed into my eyes and hers met me at my heart. She spoke to us directly in Mazatec and her daughter translated into Spanish. Occasionally doña Maria would say something to us in broken elementary Spanish, but not often. She was very accepting of us. She did not query us about why we were there; she simply invited us to be seated and wait in the hut while she went to the forest. We waited in total silence for about thirty minutes while her daughter swept the earth in the area around the hut and at the entrance doorway. After an interlude, Maria Sabina returned with fresh daisies and lilies that she had gone to pick from her garden. In her small weathered hands, she was also carrying a gourd bowl, covered by an old brown cloth.

Doña Maria approached me and wiped me repeatedly with the daisies and the lilies while she spoke prayers in Mazatec that were not translated. My eyes began to tear and I started to tremble with feeling. Then she wiped Carlo in an identical manner with the same bundle of flowers, which she held in her tiny hand. A big alligator tear fell from my cheek. Her daughter smiled at us, exposing a missing front tooth, and she explained to me that Maria was cleansing us. Maria smiled at me again, looked me up and down with impish eyes, and asked her daughter to bring in a gourd of fresh water. Doña Maria cleansed us again with the flowers, this time dipping the petals and wiping us with the dewy blossoms.

Maria Sabina turned, placed the flowers on a hewn stone altar behind her, and removed the cloth from the gourd bowl to reveal fresh psychotropic mushrooms that she called *nixti*, which means "little children," her daughter told us, fresh mushrooms from the forest that she had gone to collect. Her daughter said that it was late in the season for *honguitos*, which means "little wild mushrooms" in Spanish, but that Maria was wise about where to search and could almost always find a few. We were going to be asked to ingest a small quantity as a token sacrament to honor the energies of our visit there.

With that, doña Maria began to pray with the gourd bowl in her hands. She did not let me look into the bowl directly at the mushrooms, so I didn't actually see them clearly. This was a first step, an initiation, she instructed. Later in my life there might be more to come for me. She separated two tiny, newly sprouting baby mushrooms from the base of one very large one, which was the length of her hand. I could barely see the long grayish brown stem in her fingers. She admonished us to remember that sacred mushrooms are a sacrament always to be ingested in pairs, like the sacred twins, as we had come to her house in a pair together. She asked me to open my mouth and she placed the two minute mushroom bodies on the tip of my tongue like a communion wafer. I could feel that each one was about the size of a baby lentil bean. She requested that I swallow them.

She gave Carlo two very large mushrooms, easily the length of her palm, and asked for him to eat everything, the entire adult bodies—stem, cap, base, and all. She requested that he turn his back to me while he ingested them so that I could not observe his mushrooms or the process he underwent to consume them. Then she positioned us back-to-back on a stone bench in front of her stone altar, while she chanted and prayed over us.

Daylight was streaming into the hut and I kept observing clouds floating past the doorway during her songs and prayers. It was very obvious that mushrooms and prayers were all this blessed woman had to offer to us. The village was very poor but it was rich in an exalted, lofty perspective and in spirit. Carlo's back became quite hot as we sat there together and I began to sense an energy coming from his unseen experiences, which was fusing us into one perception. Our energy was merging some-how like the daylight and the drifting, glowing clouds, and I had the distinct impression that we were Seeing as one being, Seeing together. We were gazing energetically into the empty luminous core of existence from those vast mountain peaks and canyons, and the sunny nimbus of Huautla de Jimenez.

We sat back-to-back on the bench together, relaxing our backs into each other, and from that stone seat our subjectivity intertwined, interlaced through our mutually supporting spines. We were like the four eyes of a winged caduceus seeing in a 360-degree circle, as in the Diné prayer: beauty before us, beauty behind us, beauty below us, beauty above us, beauty all around us. My awareness floated ecstatically out through the doorway and merged with the soaring condors in the canyon, spiraling and gliding on the updrafts of a vortex, an energy cone formed by the wind, altitude, sun, and mountains. I became almost dizzy and an inner light began to shine in my forehead. I felt myself as a luminous egg, or like the sun inside a passing cloud, and I lifted up as a vapor wafts from out of the crown of my head.

At that moment a brilliant hummingbird flew in through the doorway, standing still in the air with buzzing wings, fluttering in front of my face and then flying up and darting backward before my eyes. In an instant, I must have passed out or gone into a trance. I simply left my body with the hummingbird. There was nothing but a brilliant golden white light everywhere and I could perceive Carlo's supporting awareness as a luminous cocoon of identity within all the endless existential sentient luminosity.

The next thing I remember is sitting on the bench looking at Maria Sabina's smiling little face in the sunlight, and her daughter dabbing my forehead with fresh water and flowers. They asked Carlo to take me for a walk outside the village, along the rim of the mountain overlooking the canyon, so that I could be in the elements, steady myself again out in the sunshine and fresh air, and make contact with the grounding energy of the Earth.

Carlo looked at me curiously as we walked. His stride was mildly supportive.

"Where did you go?" he asked me enthusiastically with characteristic insistence. His steps were ebullient and excited. His eyes were animated. The way he exaggerated the word "go" and the expression in his eyes made me laugh. "Something in you disappeared," he emphasized. He was happy. It was visible.

"Can you talk about it? Can you tell me where you were?" His gestures were imperative and deliberate, almost like the histrionics of a silent film star who could communicate volumes without words.

I thoughtfully described my experience to him, totally, exactly as it had occurred. I did not embellish it or make an effort to analyze.

"Wowie! Whew!" he whistled, raising his thin brows and rolling his eyes. He looked at me and looked away and then looked back again, over and over, smiling and shaking his head. Carlo found a place for me to sit and come to myself again, a nice stable rocky ledge by the edge of the canyon. Then he left me for a moment to privately express his gratitude to Maria Sabina for her graciousness. "Now don't jump," he joked. "Don't fly away from here into the canyon! Not yet!"

He was gone for a while. I completely lost track of time and history sitting there. I couldn't even imagine what it would be like to live in such a "high" place on a continual basis, so I gave myself up to eternity there. I have no idea how long he was gone and when he returned I hadn't had a single thought. I was staring at the light shift in the open chasm. The being that came back, the "she" who was sitting there, was not the "myself" that had struggled for days to get up the mountain.

When we left the village, there was no car sickness coming down, and what had taken us over a day's drive to accomplish on the way up took us only three hours on the return trip. We were not speeding in the car. Carlo insisted that time had been affected somehow with the vastness of those perceptions. We drove in silent amazement. Light speed had been reached and surpassed and had released us from some barrier that formerly weighed upon us. All time was relative and we were travelers within it, outside it, and beyond it.

We stopped in the little town of Tehuacán in the state of Puebla for several days afterward to adjust and recuperate. It was a lovely place, famous for the caves where the world's oldest cultivated corn had been found, dating back over twelve thousand years before the Christian era, and locally known for some of the world's best mineral water and springs. The climate there is just an eternal Eden and we spent the delightful days basking.

"You're a mystic," Carlo pronounced one night over our leisurely dinner in an outdoor cafe of the Tehuacán town square. "As energy, you're like a pure, still, and unfathomable lake filled with the sky. Where does the poetry in that lake come from? Are you aware of that place? You seem to me like an artist who is without any art supplies or like a weaver without a loom. I think that Dreaming and Seeing must be your art. I understand now why don Juan and doña Celestina have taken such an interest in you and why you are so at home among Native people. I'll admit that I was curious about that," he confessed. He put his elbow on the table. "You are not like everyone else here." He rested his chin in his palm and moved his eyes around the scenery to light upon all the areas surrounding us. "Do you feel it? You are nonordinary. This life must not seem like 'life' to you. Don Juan and doña Celestina must surely want to make you strong so that you can survive with all of your qualities intact in the myriad worlds in which we must all now exist. What are you doing in a place like this? I can't believe that I have found something like you here. Do you have any clue as to where you are?"

Behind his words I felt love, pure love. "You are very eloquent and I'm touched, truly. Yet, part of what you say sounds like a line from an old movie to me," I joked. "'What's a nice girl like you doing in a place like this?' The tone of your monologue was exquisite, though, and I thank you for it, profoundly."

Carlo winced, tossed his head, and caught all the innuendo. He was no one to challenge at conversation, but I always did so in my own way. "Are you a nice girl?" he insisted. "Or are you something else, *querida*? You've had experiences that don't form a part of the world you are in. I reiterate, seriously, what are you doing here?"

"How can I answer a question like that?" I snapped without meaning to, as though he had touched a chord.

"I don't mean you any harm." He grinned and paused. "I understand that one doesn't ask a magical deer why it walks in the forest. But think!" he insisted. "Where are you from, really?"

"Well, let's put the shoe on the other foot," I challenged. "What are *you* doing here?"

"I'm stuck," he confessed honestly. "I'm fighting for my life and my sanity. I'm trying to get out. I'm working hard. I'm looking for my freedom and a little happiness on the way. I'm exploring perception all along the journey."

The direct, frank honesty of his words was humbling. They stilled me. He wasn't ashamed of his angst. I was deeply emboldened and silenced by his courage, his sincerity, and his candor. I felt ashamed of snapping. It was childish. I was touched and I felt tears welling up.

"Are you lost?" he asked. "What hurt you? Do you know the way out? Are you a fellow traveler on the road? Are you an angel? Have you come here to do battle or to do something wonderful, marvelous, and extraordinary?"

His question was so profound that I couldn't offer a casual answer. I couldn't answer at all. All I remembered was my childhood playing alone in the basement and the endless whispering. He had gone to that place. "No, I'm not lost, and everything hurts at one time or another," I said from that place of my earliest trance. "I'm here with something new. I'm here to offer. And

I see incredible things, suffering and tragedy, confusion, delusion and struggle—also great beauty, delight, unknown facility, and many worthwhile wonders. I must be here to live and die, just like everyone else, I suppose."

"No," Carlo said, "not like everyone else."

"What do you mean? Well, what about you?" I challenged again. "Do you think that everyone seeks and probes the way you do? You install yourself in other realities. Most people just accept their hypnosis. You are not going to live and die like everyone else either," I summed up, satisfied with my discernment and pronouncement.

Carlo winced again, this time with more vulnerability. "We're a couple of odd ducks," he admitted. "I think that the best place to swim is between all the struggle, the suffering and the beauty, between the conflicts and peace, between the religions and traditions and dogmas; in the midst of life and of death, in the world but not of it, in between the worlds and their rules, agreements, perceptions, cognition, and glosses. That way we have a chance to arrive at what might be real, what might be our own, never overly convinced or sold on it and then shattered, never fully buying in, totally invested or lodged too far on one side. I'm not an academic, objective, intellectual skeptic, and nor am I naive. It is abstract, but I also think that it is a point of fluidity and balance. Despite how it may appear, I do not deliberately seek the deluded, nor the coveted top positions of knowledge for myself, and simultaneously I don't capitulate into the bottomless indulgence and ignorance of allowing utter oppression. I bolster myself with everything I've got, and I'm empty all the same. That is my way of being a warrior in this infinite sea of being."

I took a deep breath at the presentation of his ideas.

"Your way seems to be a transcendent, essential experience," he went on, propelled by pure ideas. "You distill and find harmony in even the most blatant paradox. My method is that of going in between the worlds. Yours is of going beyond them. Each way has the capacity to see through the illusion, but your way takes you out of all this, whereas mine takes me through another section of the labyrinth. And I would still like to ask you and for you to tell me, where do you go when you go your way?"

"Out, just out," I said.

"Most beings can't get out," Carlo pushed. "That is why you're unusual. That's also why every one of them struggles for equilibrium or dominance and advantage. Do you understand that? That's why there are endless wars, competitions, and all the opportunism and exploitation. How do you get out? How do you do it? Once you do it, what then? Perhaps you were never in. Perhaps you've come in from somewhere else. But I think that it would change things for the better in all these worlds if others could even glimpse that there are these possibilities to get out. So don't answer me now. I'd like for you to think about this for a long time. That would really be something useful, something worth sharing—if you could arrive at the ability to express your method lucidly, scientifically, or artistically, or develop the intent to guide and advise others concerning exit. Do you know what I'm talking about? Would you be willing to work on and share something like that?"

He had a way of bringing me to the brink of existential possibilities, serious seminal thought, total internal silence, utter speechlessness, and clear articulation. I did understand what he meant but I had never heard someone make such a request, or express such yearning. It was worth contemplative theory and practice. He was telling the truth. He was stuck, almost but not quite carried away, searching and pleading and calling out to the vastness, without self-pity. I admired his bravery.

A few days after that we left for Mexico City to visit the Tibetan monks. Whatever appointments Carlo previously had in Oaxaca were completely redirected by our visit together with Maria Sabina. On the drive to the capital city, Carlo restated his request and his intent. "I'm totally serious and sincere," he said. "If you would ever talk with me about these matters, I'd never look back." I understood that and I had the sense that there was something very deep compelling him, something still unexpressed, a profound loss, or a need or an injury underlying all of this.

The Tibetan monks seemed to understand the unspoken existential condition. Their way of being was to agree with the intent of liberation on a massive collective scale, and it was good, quite pleasurable in fact, to be in their company again. From the Tibetans I learned that one may attain liberation individually, but one always has the choice to offer one's wisdom to facilitate the liberation of others. That is a worthy and a profound consideration.

While Carlo was visiting with the Tibetan physician in the same tranquil suburban house as our first visit, the lama who had spoken to me and lent me books previously came into the living room where I waited. He selected a book for me to read again. On this occasion, the book was about a phenomenon the Tibetan culture calls the *delog*. These are rare and unusual beings who are resurrected from the dead in some manner after having an experience of the netherworld. They return to life to serve as guides, and they eventually become religious teachers. I wondered if this was what I had truly come from.

The monk also brought me a tiny amulet in exchange for which I made a contribution to their work in exile. There was a small paper enclosed with the amulet that explained that it contained blessed seeds and prayers from their sacred oracle. On one side of the amulet was the Kalachakra seed syllable. The paper indicated that this represents the essence of the teachings that allow beings to sail clear of the worlds of delusion, toward freedom. The design of the Kalachakra teaching was to be seen as a kind of lifeboat, a Noah's ark of realization, sailing onward with those who have been rescued and blessed toward the central sacred axis mountain, away from the levies of delusional existence and suffering, to liberation and enlightenment. On the reverse side of the amulet was a double *dorje*. This is a symbol of crossing lightning bolts, which represents an indestructible center.

The monk sat down on a futon sofa near me. "The seed will grow," he said when I opened the little envelope containing the amulet. He smiled and indicated that I should wear it near my heart, preferably hung around my neck and worn discreetly under my clothing. He laughed like a small child when I examined it, and then he got up quietly to go and see to something in another room.

Carlo's second appointment with the Tibetan doctor lasted longer than the first. When he returned to the living room he was smiling, though a little shaken, and he wanted to get right back on the road. We drove with a vengeance late into the night and we finally stopped in the state of Querétaro, another Mexican area well known for its healing springs. There was only one room available in the quaint hotel we selected, but it had two twin beds. We decided on it and were very respectful of each other, gracefully deferring to each other's modesty and sensibilities for privacy. We took turns and each sat alone in the flowering fountain courtyard listening to the night birds while the other dressed for bed.

When I returned from the courtyard into the colorfully tiled and dark-woodworked bedroom, Carlo was sitting on one bed, which he had moved slightly so that the head was toward the east wall. That would be his bed for the night. My bed was by the window with the head facing south. I always selected either of those two directions for my Dreaming. A soft breeze was gently flowing into the room, creating a fresh, tranquil feeling.

"Would you help me with something?" Carlo asked as he stood and adjusted a dim light on his bedside table.

"What?" I replied somewhat suspiciously, sitting down on my bed.

Carlo turned and smirked. He was dressed in an elegant set of midnight blue oriental silk pajamas. "Dreaming," he said. He paused for the sake of sobriety. When that had settled in to become our unshakable foundation, he went on. "I have a problem with nightmares. I don't want you to become frightened if I am startled awake or cry out during the night."

I clutched at the front of my dusky golden robe. It seemed that we both liked silk. "What can I offer?" I asked.

"Go with me in there," he replied. "I'm certain you can do it. So I'll trust you, on the quiet. That's a challenge for me. But this is it, I'm sure of it. I can't seem to find my way out and this is my last shot," he said matter-of-factly as he sat down on the edge of his bed again.

I sensed a fragility in the request and I decided to treat it like fine lace. "All right," I said. Nothing else was needed. I took a deep breath and we turned off our lights. I lay in bed feeling the most extraordinary presence in the room. Carlo's awareness became almost as engulfing as the warm night itself. It came in waves, reminiscent of the seashore with the tide coming in, closer and closer, then rolling over me and continuing to come in until I was pulled out deeper and deeper. The depth and the distance from shore became astonishing, totally indescribable, and it kept going out. Finally I sensed myself as far as one can be out to sea and at the very bottom of the deep ocean. I was in a trance then and soon I was Dreaming.

I awakened into Dreaming at the bottom of the ocean in the dark. Carlo's hand touched mine lightly. It was a tender, happy touch. We were glad to have found each other in the dark, rather like two children playing the underwater game of Marco Polo. I wondered if he was a good swimmer. He seemed totally at home and yet abandoned, playful yet lost, and purposeful all at the same instant. I could draw my breath down there directly from the awareness of my energy body within the Dream. I wondered at it. It was like being in the womb, but not so confining, or like the breathless state that some advanced Yogis experience. I pondered the possibility that Carlo might not be able to breathe. Not being able to get one's breath is often the cause of night panics. So I shared my inner breath with him down there.

I started to ascend naturally and indicated with gentle ripples of my hands and with my thoughts that Carlo should make an effort to do the same with me. He didn't seem to want to, and yet he was willing to do it because I asked it of him. We swam up together. I found a floating piece of wood for us to use like a paddleboard. We intended our way upward and upon reaching the surface, we paddle-kicked along until we arrived at a small island, all alone out in the middle of the ocean. The surrounding calm dark sea was a deep crimson color around the shore and the solitary land mass had one massive mountain peak, which shone out like the blackest obsidian, crowned with a silvery white halo cloud, against the dark pitch of the night sky.

We admired the beauty for some time and made that island our base. We were totally alone there. The mountain was topped with a stunning mirrorlike lake, and from the summit we could see the dark sea in every direction. From that island we entered into a vast coral labyrinth as we began to intend travel toward a mainland shore. Much of the labyrinth through the sea was more like a cavernous system of underground tunnels and catacombs. We were journeying together there for what seemed like an eternity, moving onward and farther. It was worth wondering if we would ever get out and although it seemed that we never would, I had no doubt that we could and would do so.

It also became obvious to me that Carlo was here on a continual basis and that he at times panicked or worried that he would not come to a place where he could lift himself up, or lift his head out of it, if he needed to. In places and at times it was quite claustrophobic and oppressive in the coral labyrinth. Carlo was searching in there. Every now and again we would come to a dead end and then we'd have to backtrack through another skinny passage and go another way, traveling sometimes at high speeds, other times at a more moderate pace, and at times at a mere creep, all in the dark of the watery depths without any light or visuals. We had to move on in this manner until we found our way by touch and by echolocation.

Carlo began to have perceptions about the nature of that reality and those perceptions moved in the water like dolphin and whale songs. They were profound insights about our condition down there. One prevailing song consisted of but one verse, "We're already dead." That song followed him everywhere like a specter or an echo, even, I surmised, into his waking everyday level of awareness, which must have seemed quite like what the Tibetans call the *bardo*, a veritable carnival of delusions and ghosts through which the awareness of a departed being travels, searching for another birth or an exit.

I would counter that song with transcendent love songs or comedy, like my "So what?" responsory, which seemed to come naturally to me. From time to time Carlo would come to our rescue and find a little hole for us to crawl or swim through, or I would find a place that had an open roof from which we could ascend to see the sky. When we finally did arrive at a mainland shore, the world we encountered there was like a freak show. The activities of the inhabitants at that level of reality consisted of nothing but cannibalizing each other and serving up cannibal feasts, plus the consumption of and the hunger for any synthetic existence including plastics, drugs, and even false imagery induced by hypnosis.

They were all terrified of war and they added to that diet the unstable sale and the infliction of the byproducts of their synthetic, abusive, and decadent lives. They were hypnotized by televisions. This deterioration was compounded by the rape of the environment with its subsequent tacky redecoration. So to alleviate their suffering, they promoted superficial dating. It was as disgustingly horrible and trivial as anything could be, especially since most of them were eunuchs and genetic scrap-pile material.

We were both revolted to the vomiting core but the inhabi-tants kept trying to offer us "deals" and positions to stay with them and teach them. They wanted "knowledge." I insisted that if we did it, we must have high, honored standards, clean con-tracts, timely generous payments, gracious reciprocity, privacy, respect, no incurred debts, and no taxes. Naturally we weren't particularly interested in it, but I was willing to teach if we could enjoy some time together. If that wasn't possible as we would have wished under those conditions, then the answer was "no." The inhabitants were far too false and consumptive and so we decided to keep on searching.

I realized that I couldn't just leave Carlo alone out in the middle of the ocean or in that reality and still honor my promise to help him find a way out. I also discerned that it was going to take quite a lot of searching to find a place where we could both be happy and well and together, and still honor teaching requests holistically, or pleas for assistance in liberation. I was willing to go on that expedition. So I decided to look upward and I caught a shooting star that took me beyond the earthly magnetic poles. It was dark here, too, but it was a spatial dark-ness, occasionally illuminated and filled with astral mystery. From here, we would be able to observe the entire axis mundi.

Beyond this I had no clue. Carlo trusted me and was willing to do as I suggested, but I did not wish to expose him to any unnecessary suffering. I had to consider his energy and his capacities in every choice. I have crawled through the transformational trenches at times in my life, but this is not a path one would deliberately select for another, unless there is no other way out. So I decided to call don Juan. That was the best decision I could have made. I saw celestial lights coming in the blackness of space and received his response. The advice he gave to me was unexpected and it is something that is completely private between him and me, and between Carlo and me. I have since followed it to the letter, even though I can never reveal exactly what his formula for the remedy was. Suffice it to say that it has begun to work.

I awoke to the sound of one of my favorite birds, a comical black grackle cackling and mimicking on a tree branch outside the open window near the head of my bed. Dawn was coming and Carlo was tranquilly, softly snoring away in his bed. After awakening, Carlo wanted to have a serious conversation.

"Look here," he said as he finished freshening for the morning. "What you've been doing is extraordinary, seminal. You can actually Dream for others. I want to tell you something now that I never would have shared with you otherwise. My family has a history of certain illnesses and I'm trying as hard as I possibly can to escape that genetic predisposition and fate, but if I cannot do it, I would really like to come to you when I need to move on. Do you understand what I mean?"

"Do you mean when you die?" I asked, totally taken aback and touched at the same time.

"Well, we've all got to do it," he remarked with a tinge of bitterness. "I trust you. You are an energetic virtuoso free of dogma. You're innocent and compassionate. You're well educated, yet the wisdom of your instincts has not been conditioned or bred out of you. I'll let you in. You're a champion."

"You make me sound like a racehorse."

"Hold your horses," he said, "but I know where to place my bets and I understand when to let go of the reins and let the horse take over the race. You'll win, I'm sure of it. You won't have an easy time with me. Oh, and they won't make it easy for you. They'll throw everything they've got at you and you'll sidestep it all. If you have to fight, you'll look defenseless and throw thunderbolts. This won't be a cakewalk. So this is something I'd like to keep just between us until we're out of the woods. Then afterward, if you have a mind for it, you can say whatever you wish and you might even have a care for those others. This will be your test flight. We are talking about a forever intent that transcends death. I'll do my part, whatever it takes. That's forever. I need a little help and it's as simple as that. I've worked very hard. I'll provide you with every resource I have left to offer that amounts to anything in such a request. Believe me, I've tried them all. I've had those opportunities. You're it."

"This is the strangest request that anyone has ever made of me, but I really think I understand what you're talking about," I said, astonished.

"Enough said," he concluded.

Twilight Navigation

1. Intend a meeting place to go and visit in Dreaming. You must first select others to meet. Then agree with the other members of your "Dream Team" that all of you will participate.

2. Select the agreed-upon place. It is best to begin with a place that you can actually visit physically. Start simply. Do not select a sacred place that requires a special kind of energetic permission. Begin somewhere cheerful, nurturing, pleasant, and safe, close by and quiet, like a small children's park or a garden.

3. Now visit the place physically. Everyone on the Dream Team should become familiar with all of the everyday details, plus have respectful awareness of the nonordinary nuances and energies present there. Visit the place often. You may even make humble offerings of seeds, flowers, sacred smoke, or some spring water poured onto the ground. Ask permission of the place to be received and protected.

4. On each occasion of twilight navigation, enter into Dreaming at the same time as the other members of the Dream Team, if possible. Time is relative, but when you are first beginning, the act of synchronizing your intent will help the effort.

5. Don't force the process; rather, allow it to unfold. Proceed gently, step by step. Intend to see lucidly the place that you have selected at the exact time of day or night that you are

Dreaming it, or at the exact time of day you will revisit it in the waking world and be open to the presences of the other Dreamers. Reset your intent several times during an extended Dreaming session.

6. Look for clues that the other members of the Dream Team have been there, or that they are there. You may not see the others at first, but as you zero in closer and closer, you will be able to sense and track their Dreaming presences until you may actually meet. This sometimes requires multiple attempts.

7. Now in the waking world, revisit the intended place and track all the synchronicities; the moments when the Dream exists in the waking world. Use these to guide your continued Dreaming.

8. Remember, this kind of exploration is only and always done with permission and mutual consent. Otherwise, you will encounter energetic guardians that will prevent you, your intent, and your progress.

9 Enjoy. This is a playful, fun, and useful practice that we work with often at our teaching events. Over time, many of our participants become very good at some of the basic foundations of Dreaming, and discover many creative applications.

10. Once you can actually meet one another in Dreaming as energy and awareness, and can confirm this, there are many more advanced possibilities that may open to you.

Part Two

Wisdom
and Applications

7

Lessons from a Firebird Beyond Death

Doña Celestina had a long talk with me when I returned from the journey of initiation with Carlo, a talk that would guide me for the rest of my life. "There is going to come a time," she said, "when you will have to put everything that you are learning into practice as an aspect of your very existence. You'll see it. You'll live it. It will be serious, life or death."

We were sitting on her front porch watching the desert twilight. Wild rabbits were running under the creosote bushes and hopping around in the mesquite scrub. Every element of the scenery was tinged with dark green, purple, and black.

"You're going to go far in this work," she continued. "I'm sure that you will go down deeper into Mexico again to work with other shamans and healers, and you'll also need to continue with your Western education. All of the things we are asking for you to learn to do, there is a reason for it, and that is so you will do them. You may become liberated and realized in life, as you have spoken of with me, and that means facing all of the myriad things that hold beings back: fear, horror, illness, struggle, envy, idiocy, falsehood, wrath, and death.

"You might—I say you *will*—triumph over it all eventually, because you are stronger than you even imagine. So you'll be called upon to act with what you have been given. Those who are given much are challenged to act in a manner that is worthy of what they have received. For you, that means everything. Each of us has given you a task—don Juan, myself, and now even Carlo—and you must take what we have given you seriously, for it is not all for nothing that we are sharing with you. You'll learn. If you attain what you seek, you may later be called upon to teach or to act in an energetic capacity on the behalf of others.

"It is necessary to see death to really understand the challenge it poses. It is all well and good to talk about death from a safe and comfortable distance—I'll do this or that—but to look death in the eye is quite another matter, and to look death in the eye with victory, to have that victory over it, or to navigate well at the moment of death is yet another. Death, like love, catches most quite unprepared. It takes many forms and it is intimate with each individual it comes to.

"Then there is the issue of living. What can possibly motivate such a lifelong fire and flight? I see you are an ace, a real resurrection, but what will get you into the air? I have heard it said that those who have something to die for also have something to live for, and for you that means something to soar for. I would like for you to think long and well on that."

I think about that statement every day. Not a moment goes by that I do not examine my existence within that template. As the Native peoples say, my heart soars like a hawk. All of those words she uttered came true. I saw more death. I saw what rises from it. I had something to live for and something to die for. Carlo, don Juan, and doña Celestina, and all of my ancestors, had made sure of that and had all set the stage for what was to come.

Over the years that followed, I traveled deeply into Mexico and studied with other shamans and energy healers. I obtained my master's degree in education. I faced the trials of near death and overcame them. I began to teach. I explored and developed Dreaming, listening to the Twilight Language and following its guidance. And then I reached yet another level, another layer of the onion.

I had maintained contact with them all—don Juan, doña Celestina, and Carlo—through my Dreaming and through letters and postcards while I worked on my degree. I was offered a teaching position, which I accepted because it was part of the task that doña Celestina had prescribed. I walked a path of intent, and worked earnestly toward eventual liberation. Yet something was chewing away at me. While I was endeavoring in my teaching position, I became aware that Carlo was struggling and that don Juan was preparing to leave the world, but neither of them had called me energetically yet and their intent required the sudden dynamic of the war cry. I persevered with the preparations, the responsibilities, and the trust they had placed in me.

Then the call came. Almost simultaneously, I received profound messages in Dreaming from each of them. One morning as I lay in bed, a lightning bolt came right into my Dreaming through my head. The entire scene exploded and dissolved and was replaced by the afterglow of the bolt. Where the lightning had struck, there was a blue ball of fire, and from within that ball of fire I saw don Juan glowing as if he were made of pure electricity and ether. I understood immediately that he had come from the Celestial realms and that he was telling me I would no longer find him in a body on Earth in the way I had formerly done. My human form vanished right then and I went with him energetically beyond this world.

But the part of me that still needed to live out my life and be of service remained. No sooner had that shock struck, and while what was left of me was trying to stabilize, I received a copy of Carlo's most recent book in the mail, lovingly sent in an

unmarked manila envelope. It had been a long time since Carlo
had published anything about his shamanic work and I understood that this was a message. The voice didn't sound like the
excited, sweet, and intrigued Carlo. The tone of the text was
without joy—reclusive, angry, lost, stuck, and sad. I realized
immediately that he was ill.

As I was agonizing and contemplating how to proceed, I was
called yet again in Dreaming and given a third, imperative indi-
cation that I should come right away, this time from doña
Celestina's quadrant. I made all the necessary arrangements and
followed the call almost immediately. The result was that I
would be put to the ultimate tests of love and awareness beyond
death. I had to overcome and alchemize my emotions, and use
them all at the same time. I had to act fast and be strong, radical,
unconventional, and yet gentle. And I certainly learned more
about death. I was trusted and allowed to go in and navigate.

What is it like? It is like being eaten by vultures on one level.
The dying being may balance that with generosity, affection, and
compassion. It is like following a light through a dark labyrinth
on another level. The body becomes very cold and you can't get
warm through ordinary means, such as blankets. It requires
inner warmth and inner light. It is like becoming the last sentient
being left alone to pray in a cemetery. It is like making love to
pieces of a dismembered corpse as they shut down, in order to
raise them. For some beings, it is like searching for a lit match in
a void of black darkness, and like being a luminous balloon on a
cord that you let go for others—and then you are the balloon
and not the one letting go. There are many places where the
departing awareness may travel, depending on the level of preparedness and the willingness to release and transmute negative
emotions and mental stains before death. I became a sojourner
into that transition and into those domains.

There is no way to describe the difference between the

preparation for this task and the actual experience; the living and dying and resurrecting are much bigger than talking, recounting, and practicing. Navigating the departing awareness toward a good place is different from going through the processes that lead to death and accepting. There are better places to go and there is no reason to cause fear, suffering, and panic. Those states are engendered by attachment. We are inherently blessed with our natural luminous awareness, if we can find it. Some beings never lose their way to that. So far, I have not. I have been told that I never shall. There are guides for the dying that are prepared by energy itself, guides who understand what is required. When it is all over, all of the places can be good if we are together with those we love in an ultimate sense that leads to enlightenment and liberation. Heaven and hell are a state of mind.

My service and assistance, which had been requested in this call, did indeed lead to that place that doña Celestina had spoken of so often, that of finally standing on my own as a woman of wisdom with love, and power, and allies. Even though mourning is a very hard thing, it is bearable if we offer it up, and joy, love, and freedom can be found. I paraphrase a line from a favorite story, spoken by one beloved to another, that expresses it well: "I would rather be a sad spirit by your side, than enter into heaven without you, my love." The other says, "No, use your last breath to find illumination and liberation."

Who can say which path is best? Who can judge? There are so many possibilities. Can we fly freely on the wings of intent? Can we be pathfinders of uncharted territory? Can we do so in a way that does not harm those we love or the freedom we love? Yes.

As I mourned, I wrote and published books to assist me in the grieving, healing, and transformational process, and to empower others. The result was that I began to receive invitations to teach Dreaming. I was an energetic widow now, but joined from within, and as I came out of it, I accepted invitations to speak at symposiums, in conferences, and on panels dealing with shamanism, healing, love, and alternative and traditional Western medicine. I spoke on remaining happy and stable in the face of suffering and on transforming our challenges into victories. All of this materialized by energy's design, not my own, as if out of the blue.

Then I started receiving requests for private consultations, and from that work, I began to develop the body of energetic practices that don Juan, doña Celestina, and Carlo had requested I formulate for the benefit of others. I was sought out by psychologists and psychiatrists, medical doctors, sexual therapists, counselors working with death and dying, energy workers, shamans, healers, and scientists. My caseload became quite large but the energy kept moving on a more massive scale. I accumulated data regarding coma and death and an infinite array of maladies, traumas, and conditions—data that continues to grow.

I found in each case that the Twilight Language of Dreaming gave me an avenue for understanding the energetic gateways of the maladies and conditions and the exits from them. More than accumulating data, I accumulated experience. This work is a mixture of moving the energy directly and skillfully with permission—subtly yet powerfully, gently and with love and wisdom, no strings attached—and of providing the educational experience that is sought after by those who wish or need to learn to understand, those who would like to or who must navigate for themselves.

The degree to which an individual or a collective holds on to a condition is in fact indicative of the depth of learning that is sought or needed. Their education follows suit. The more they hold on, the more they are trying to or are required to learn for themselves. At the same time, the more energetic assistance, and perhaps the more containment or revelation they may need. Everything is interlaced. Thus after a threshold of trying to learn is reached, and after the energy has been moved, a realization and a result will follow. If the needed realization and learning truly come, once the energy has been moved, something will then be released, often forever.

This energy work has released me from deeply life-threatening conditions, and so it is profound, grounded, and celestial. There are many types of energetic maladies but all of them arise from the collective and individual delusions that we inflict. Our suffering is a direct byproduct of the way that the entire Tree of Life exchanges energy. Rather like the fallen tower of Babel, our fractionated nature is due to our lesser comprehension of, misunderstanding of, and misconduct regarding ultimate intent. Most maladies are caused by one simple factor: inappropriate reciprocity. This creates conditions from which imbalances, ills, and delusions dependently arise.

As an example, you can go all the way back to the mythological Eve if you wish. If she just hadn't reached for that fruit . . . It was an inappropriate and petty exchange of energy after such an Eden had been given. Instead of releasing herself first into the reciprocal ecstasy and magnifying generosity of appreciation, perhaps even love, and then asking for and receiving the gradual blessing she lacked, that of understanding the taboo at her level of awareness, she did something else. She coveted and she misinterpreted. The medicine was to be a greater love than that, and a more humble one. The medicine was to reciprocate love without attachment or false knowledge. Realization was still to come. It was never only about Adam, or about Eve, or the serpent, or the Tree of Knowledge. It was about from whence it all came.

This is a metaphor for the whole of life. Everyone wants his or her premature unrealized cut. It is the decadent opportunism of each being or collective, pursuing its own puny or grandiose vision. The result is that those cuts are inflicted and reciprocal conditions are caused and then multiplied. Every action has an equal and opposite reaction plus a consequence and a cause, so one must work in harmony and be careful which door one leans against. Otherwise one creates imbalance. There is more than enough universal energy for harmony, but even chaos has uplifting evolutionary intent. That is truly holistic. So the key to finding the exit for any condition is to find the points of inappropriate reciprocity. To do that, the three levels of the Tree of Life must be addressed: the Underworld, the Earth, and the Celestial.

The first actual case that came to me was selected by doña Celestina herself. The client was a Papago Indian gentleman residing in a nearby Sonoran village who was a longtime alcoholic and as a result had developed poor circulation and diabetic gout in his right leg. I had to Dream with this man for a while to find the sources of his trauma. He had been left without parents at an early age and had little starting income. He had no formal education; he was self-taught and taught by life. He was practically a genius, very eloquent, but also a lovable drunk and he would not stop drinking. Even as an elder, he was strong, handsome, and hardworking, very clean. He had no place to lay his head at night, no home, and yet he camped outside in the pleasant Mexican climate and bathed in one set of clothes each day at an outdoor spigot. He would change into another set of clothes afterward, which he kept clean and safely stashed all about town, and then he'd ask permission to hang his wet clothing on someone's line to dry, in exchange for which he would clean up their yard. He gained his meals and spending money doing all sorts of odd jobs. And that was his existence.

The only woman he had ever loved was a young school-teacher who had left him, and he lamented this all of his life. He told me that she was very pretty and he missed her terribly all of the time. He said that was why he was a drunk. He had no wife, no children, and no family. He had been even more of a loner ever since she left him. He bonded with me immediately and asked me to stay with him and he told me that he loved me, but he said that he wasn't going to marry me because he only wanted to marry her. I observed him and accompanied him during his daily activities because he asked me to, and because doing so was necessary in order to discern his malady. He liked to shout at the top of his lungs to all of the townspeople and he would rant about the state of the world while he brought everyone in the tiny village the local paper. He told me that he thought he would die in the street, that it was his fate and he did not care. He was going to live his life independently, as he saw fit, come what may. He defended his integrity, saying that the only fault he had was the drinking, that otherwise he had led a clean life, so he was not afraid to meet his end working up to the last moment.

The cause of his delirium was semen, without enough meditation and orgasmic ecstasy, which had gone to his brain. This is the reason that many men become alcoholics. They wish to rise out of a disappointment or something else and toward another end they struggle excessively with their body or their circumstances, which will not allow them to fully reach what they seek. The alcohol, which acts at first like more semen rising to the head, gives them a sense of uplifting release for a time; they strive, and then they become drunk and begin to crash. With each new occurrence the brain becomes more congested and the bodily organs follow. With each crash there is more destabilization and less liftoff. Both sides of his body were affected, but it was the right side that manifested the malady at that time. Diabetics store the seminal energy, which should be love in a healthy world, as the energy replacement, sugar. If the male energy is very seminal, there is a tendency toward sugar-related conditions. Alcohol, of course, converts to pure sugar in the bloodstream, and it takes a good disciplinarian liver to hold down the ruckus.

Having found the points of lack of reciprocity, I transformed my energy body into an energetic distillery and manufactured an energetic elixir of ecstatic orgasmic intent. And then one night I was able to address the issue of his leg, which the local doctors were threatening to amputate, fearing that it would eventually become gangrenous. I had the man, whose name was Mauricio, lie down and Dream under the full moon. While he was asleep and in Dreaming, with his permission, I entered into an awakened Dream, and, via the moonlight, I went into his body and put the energy of love that he was missing back into his leg. Within three weeks, the leg, which had been swollen and black and for which the doctors could do nothing, was returned to normal size and color, with only a mild skin condition remaining. The serpent energy is so imbalanced in the collective world at present that the shedding of skin conditions is one thing for which I cannot yet completely provide remedy.

Mauricio was quite surprised and delighted with his new leg. The kind local doctor was justly amazed. Small Mexican village inhabitants often accept such healings as miraculous. It took Mauricio a very long time, however, to come to the next level of realization. Still transferring all his affection to me, he told me that he loved me dearly but that he was certain I would leave him now, and even though we had shared those experiences, he would rather give me up than stop drinking. The villagers thought it would kill him to give me up. To these people, I had become like his local sidekick, going with him everywhere while he recounted his life story to me and shouted at the townsfolk. They knew nothing about me and thought I was a sweethearted fool or an innocent saint sent by God to their village.

This misinterpretive mystique was totally necessary, doña Celestina assured me, and was often essential to fully enter in and do the work. "They will all see you through their eyes," she said. "They can't see you."

To me there was no mystique. Regardless of whatever history I had, I sincerely meant it when I told Mauricio that I loved him too and would not leave him, but the whole village insisted that I do so, because they felt that it was the only way for him to realize or make a final choice. They decided to let him die. They actually took me away from him like snatching a pacifier away from a toddler. It was a village conspiracy. I was invited to stay in homes instead of out under the stars with him and he was not allowed to visit, especially if he was coming drunk. So my truthful promise took on an ultimate meaning. It was not until he was ready to die that he asked for me, and he told me then that there were some things he would like to change.

The Twilight Language of Dreaming has shown me ways of entering into many conditions and thus into the beings that have them. This is only done with permission, which is the etiquette. It has allowed passage into coma and death, sexual dysfunction, autism, psychosis and schizophrenia, physical illness, emotional disorders, grief, anger, traumatic stress disorders, and obsessions and compulsions, and it has proven itself as a vehicle for the retrieval of parts of our being that become lost.

Another case, and a simpler one, was that of a Spaniard named Francisco. He was an anthropologist that I encountered while I was back in the Huichol's land attending a ceremony to which I had been invited. He was traveling there with a team of photographers and social scientists intent on recording the ceremony. We were all staying in the local clinic's bunkhouse, which was designed for the regional health care workers who visited periodically. Their team had ridden into that part of the mountainous canyon on horseback and this fellow had been kicked in the groin by his mule while he was trying to mount it.

We were the last two awake in the bunkhouse on the night before the ceremony. We were sitting at the worktable talking and sipping tea when he began to complain about his swollen, sore testicle. He told me the whole story of how he had been kicked. In classic Spanish fashion, he couldn't understand what the mule had against him mounting! I was beside myself watching him whine, but he insisted that it was very painful and wanted to strip himself of his denim trousers to show me the bruise. Once I saw his underwear being revealed, I didn't want to look further, but he requested that I do so. There was a large, raised, angry bruise on the inside thigh at the juncture with the groin that was going to turn blue-black and nasty during the night.

I contemplated the potential complications. We had some dried fruits sitting out on the table and without thinking twice, I selected a large fig from the wooden bowl and bit the fruit into the shape of his bruise. Then I told him to dip that fig into the hot tea and to place that directly onto the sore area. To my amazement he did so, and he began to marvel at how good it felt. In the morning he was jumping around with glee. The testicle was as right as rain. The condition was balanced and he felt differently, too. It was a miracle! The bruise had completely disappeared and the swelling was all gone. There was no pain remaining whatsoever. It was a profound case of sympathetic healing and empathy. He was not ever going to mistreat his testicle again! Francisco was now in search of understanding.

He showed himself to the socialized medical doctor, head of the regionally coordinated Huichol medical services, who was in the village on a routine visit and to attend the ceremony. The doctor had seen the injury before and after and had prescribed no Western treatment, as none was available in the village other than a warm bath. He was totally stunned by the disappearance of the injury, which he had told Francisco might take as long as one or two weeks to calm. The doctor came to the bunkhouse, asked me to go for a walk in the village with him, and took me around introducing me to the local shamans and curers while we talked. As a result of this incident, I became a close and cherished friend of that doctor and was invited to other Huichol ceremonies.

Unfortunately for Francisco, he also had a bad front tooth that turned suddenly brown during the stay in the mountains, and he was rushed to the dentist right after the ceremony. The dentist, a woman, pulled the tooth, which was tragic and primitive. I could have fixed that, too. He came to see me later and told me that he had made a terrible mistake with his teeth. Francisco suffered from intestinal parasites as well, which is not that uncommon. I have since learned to understand, but at the time I was unfamiliar with the energetic dynamic, so I only offered dietary advice and a prescription for purification tea. All of these maladies were directly related to his relationship with sexual energy and with "knowledge." It was easy enough to See this via the Twilight Language of Dreaming, and when he invited me to do so, I was able to offer appropriate remedies.

Next there was Penelope, the captive black jaguar. I encountered her in a gypsy zoo that was traveling as a caravan to the small villages surrounding doña Celestina's home. Penelope's claws and first digits had been amputated so that her paws would be under her captor's influence and she would be unable to ravage her handlers from within her cramped cage. When I saw her, she insisted that I Dream her new digits and send them to her through Dreaming. Jaguars are fluent in the language of Dreams and for this they are often called *nagual*, or the energy being that comes from the other realms and goes back into them—the energy being that brings messages and speaks to us from Dreaming.

She called to me in Dreaming repeatedly with her persistent

demand. It took me quite a while to honor her request, not out of lack of desire, but because that trauma is a very severe and sensitive issue between the masculine and the feminine energies, and between the Tree of Knowledge and the Tree of Life. It is much like the devil's bargain made by the father of a young girl in the tale of the handless maiden. The maiden's hands are amputated and are given to the devil for his pleasure in exchange for material wealth for her father.

As a result of my finally succeeding in this favor for her, Penelope the black jaguar reciprocated with her medicine and I earned the honorary shamanic title of a *balam*, which means "jaguar" among Mayan shamans. The Mayan region of Mexico is where most of the black jaguars come from. She evidently showed herself in Dreaming to all the Mesoamerican shamans when she was restored there and the shamans then seemed to See me in that "jaguar" light. In the waking world, her digits are growing anew, very gradually.

The balam can See and stalk in the shaman's world, in the Underworld, in the dark and at night, in Dreams, and if they need to be so, they are one of the trusted guardians of all the mysteries of creation and of the ancestral realms, all the knowledge and the treasures. They can become purely energetic beings and so they do not need to reside in a physical form to be guardians. The balam are protectors, not keepers, and thus they do not insist that one with medicine remain forever in their domains. They offer good guidance when one needs to be there, if they are willing to do so, and if one can understand it. For this reason, even though I travel beyond that path, I am free to accept the offer of assistance, and I am grateful for it.

Although one may be pursuing the path of illumination, another being may be in darkness. At times we may be in either, or in both, and one must find the harmony and incorruptible passes in each. This work is a matter of reciprocating the energy properly and of accepting and receiving well what is reciprocated, thus activating what potential is there and putting what should be there into place. The source energy comes directly from the energy of which all things come, released by the appropriate intent. It is accessed through the understanding of what is intended to be there, which is conveyed via energy, by the Twilight Language of Dreaming, and through true energetic Seeing.

It is as simple as that. The Twilight Language of Dreaming is the language of the energy itself. Energy conveys all of the necessary information and conveys intent, and the sublime original intent. Thus one does not need other medicine. One simply follows the language of the energy and all of its instructions and guidance, and one receives the initiations and the results when one is ready to receive and understand. The energy is the source.

Beyond appropriate reciprocity (a concept explained in Practice Seven), the other dynamic in this work is that of Seeing through all the illusions, the element of realization. The original state of energy is empty and pure potentiality, without inherent forms. One must be able to honor the manifestation and at the same time listen to and visualize the original—not a derivative language—and understand it, in order to obtain the complete wisdom being expressed. Then one must be in a state of sacred emptiness oneself in order to See and receive any empowerments. This is why the ability to see in the dark can be useful, but one must also have the ability to see around the false light.

We are selective listeners and also selective seers, subject to imprints, and so one must begin listening and Seeing from a place of total inner silence without predisposition or prejudice to be able to really discern what one hears and Sees. Oftentimes we think we hear, or see, but we can go deeper. We think that we understand but we do not. We want to ascribe our own summary understanding to the message and the perceptions, rather than really listening to or scanning for the deepest truth, or the ultimate truth. This may be a truth that we have never allowed, or heard or seen expressed, or a truth that we are not fully ready for, communicated in a manner to which we are not accustomed, or in a way that we have never even encountered.

This is why emptiness, and speaking and understanding the language of energy, are so very important. Emptiness is more void and immaculate than a clean slate. And all being, all existence communicates via the language of energy. It transcends every other language and reaches us universally, directly. We all understand that language, even though we may not know how we do it, and we cannot turn it completely off. We are subject to it, even if we look to some other more limited source for our understanding or our experience of the world. One might call this the language of the original mind. It is free from limited cognitive systems. From the practical standpoint of healing to the vantage point of enlightenment or spirituality, these realizations become absolutely invaluable.

Practice Seven

Reciprocity

1. The principal of reciprocity is very simple. For everything that you receive, you must also give. What bank is there in the world from which you may only withdraw and never deposit? How will abundance grow that way? So it is with life and with death, and with the Underworld, the Earth, and the Celestial levels and realms. So it is with all being; thus be careful what you accept.

2. One does not have to reciprocate in a conventional manner, but one must eventually reciprocate with the distilled essence of the value of what one has received, and reciprocate in a clean manner, and reciprocate with magnifying gratitude and joy for the free opportunity to reciprocate. There is no way to cheat. One may be creative and daring and respectful. Inappropriate reciprocity causes suffering, and if one wishes to be free, one reciprocates in sublime, kind, elegant, and generous ways. A classic teaching story that expresses this well is that of the "widow's mite" in the New Testament.

   In the parable, everyone is asked to give at Temple, and all of the others in attendance criticize a widow's gift of one coin only, a measly mite. They do not see the other side of the coin, her kindness and generosity. They only see her poverty. Then Jesus scolds them all for their superficiality and tells them that in fact she has given more than all of them put together. She has given all that she has to offer in the form that is acceptable at Temple that day, and the others have given only a minute portion of all that they have. Jesus says that her gift is of more value and outweighs the other gifts in quantity and quality, potency and sincerity. This is reciprocity.

3. Energetically, the three levels of being should always be addressed in every act of reciprocation. The Underworld should receive the heavy energy, our weight, which is light, nourishing, and educational to beings at a lower level than ourselves. The Earth should receive our gratitude, affection, much effort, generosity, and feast; and the Celestial levels should receive essences and praise, love and joy if we are capable of them, offerings of spiritual intent, celebration, meditation, training of the mind, sacred exchanges of refined sexual energy, music and dance, prayer and ceremony, and our visions.

4. Our bodies naturally reciprocate the three levels, with the umbilical breath of the Underworld womb, then the newborn in-breath of Earth, followed by the out-breath of the Cosmos; and with birth, life, and death themselves. The body never lies and a failure or an imbalance in natural harmonious reciprocity results in unwellness. There is much wisdom in the body and we should praise, respect, and honor this wisdom.

5. What we forget is to engage our emotions, minds, and spirits with our natural bodily vehicle. We ignore the fact that every act should be an intended mindfulness meditation and becomes a reciprocation of something. We do not fully involve our intent, and in living our lives without intentional reciprocity, we create lives that are out of balance and of less than the desired quality.

6. The remedy for this is to begin to reciprocate the three levels with our every thought, word, and deed. Heavy Underworld energy can be offered up and consumed in a purging, transmuting fire ceremony. Earth energy may be reciprocated in myriad ways, such as stewardship and caretaking, holistic

eco-environmental efforts, protection and beautification. Spiritual energies may be reciprocated with quests, acts of boundless courage and generosity, supplications, and efforts that take us beyond the human form, such as Dreaming practices. These are only a few examples.

7. We have our precious bodies and minds to assist us in reciprocity every moment of our lives. By breathing out and evacuating our heavy energies and offering them to the Underworld to be consumed, we nourish others and purge ourselves; then by breathing in and receiving the new blessings of freshened lightness from the Mother Earth and from the Celestial realms, we feed our being, lighten our load, and prepare ourselves for our transformation. What is heavy old poison for us is light nourishment and education for beings at another level. Remember this.

8. By purging the accumulated, concentrated stagnancy from our bodies and by circulating and receiving new higher energies, we refresh ourselves. And through holding a kindness or a gratitude in our minds for everything we receive, even if it is not always to our (premature) liking, even if it is like a grain of colored sand in a windstorm, we begin to form a healthy way of transmuting and of making a pearl from that grain of sand.

9. The mindfulness meditation of continually being aware that this is the appropriate and the refined ceremony of life will bring about in our being the artistry of reciprocity. One may begin simply, but over time the gestures will concentrate into the placement of that pearlescent grain of sand within a sand mandala painting, only to release it all with blessings once the ceremony is completed.

10. There is really only one simple commandment for recovering and enhancing happiness, freedom, and well-being: *Learn to practice and begin to practice reciprocity.*

8

Illumination, Realization, and Liberation

After I began writing, I moved to a small city in the Southeast. Writing has always been a quiet affair in the South. I remained in contact with doña Celestina, who admonished me more than ever that now was the time for wise women leaders, for women writers and speakers, sacred priestesses, and women who attain realization, time even for women Buddhas who arrive at ultimate liberation on a nondiscriminatory path. Don Juan had felt that this was the moment for energetic evolution far beyond masculine and feminine halflings, and Carlo had been focused on now as the time for the evolution of perception, awareness, and thought. He wanted me to be a door opener into new experiences and possibilities, a thinker, a dynamo, a guide, and a mover of consciousness.

Needless to say, I had a lot on my plate. I searched for a home with burning intent to contemplate and an entirely new life to live. Challenges had been set before me and they required the profound source of wisdom of my ancestors, in addition to everything I had received from my mentors. I am from the eastern Cherokee lands and was raised for a time in the Creek territory. This whole area where we made our home before the American Revolution is filled with sacred places, from temple mounds where the ancient civilizations here traded in harmony with the Maya and the Toltecs, to the pristine waterfalls, natural bridges, sublime caverns, and upturned caves that transform into sacred pools; from the lush green hills, to mountains with lakes; and from the battles of the civil rights movement to the second oldest river upon the Mother Earth.

After establishing myself here, I found that Tibetan monks had also chosen this region of America, and that they had moved into the area at about the same time I did. Because of my previous experiences with them, I considered this to be significant. Within a short while, the monks founded the American seat of one of their most important monasteries nearby. They also became affiliated with one of the universities, which seemed quite relevant.

At first, some of my time here was spent visiting with them, writing, developing ideas, and doing research. I also began giving seminars. Additionally, I spoke on international panels and served as a consultant, and was invited to teach workshops, make ceremony, and even lead experiential events and sacred journeys. The presentation of new ideas was tough going at first. There is often initial resistance to change in consciousness. To bolster what I had to offer, I stepped up my efforts and increased my research in shamanism; global spirituality; sacred sexuality; nonverbal communication; mass trance and movement; the raising of global energy; transcendent, transpersonal, transformational psychology; and healing. I received occasional private appointments for energetic intervention and also traveled to Mexico quite frequently, whenever I could.

It can be said that I was totally dedicated to gratifying and necessary tasks. Yet something was still to come. Continuing with my education and myriad energetic explorations, I spent the remaining time deepening my skills in the Twilight Language of Dreaming. This gave me entry into all of my required studies.

As a result of the sincere, properly motivated, and vast outreach, I made new and wonderful contacts in the Mayan area of Mexico, so I was traveling to that region with more frequency than ever. I found that I was visiting the sacred sites there more often than I was journeying to any other section of the country.

Simultaneously, people were beginning to come from all over the world to do this work and I was receiving many invitations from both inside and outside the United States. A gracious invitation arrived in 2001 to make presentations on Dreaming, energetic offerings, and bodywork at a conference dealing with Mayan cosmology and shamanism. I decided to accept it with thanks. It was during and following that conference, while in Mérida, Yucatán, that I had a portentous experience, which began the next phase of what doña Celestina had heralded.

On the evening of the last day of this conference, which had been thoroughly enjoyable, as I casually strolled to a thank you dinner for the presenters, I passed by a small artisan's shop containing high-quality reproductions of ancient carvings. I looked in the window because I heard a little voice calling to me from that shop, insisting that I stop as I walked by.

"Tssst. Ooopa. Aren't you going to get me out of here?" the little voice said. The voice was obviously not human.

Now I'm not always given to such animistic experiences. This kind of spontaneous and extreme merging of the levels of reality, lifting the veil drastically, is quite rare and indicates an energetic presence, so if this happens I do take it very seriously. Having this kind of encounter at an academic conference was even more unusual. Entering the shop, I scoured the place for something, anything that might be calling to my Dreaming attention, but I couldn't find a single thing that seemed to actively call out to me.

I had been walking down that particular street, which I had never traveled before, after turning the final corner to approach the designated meeting place, a lovely gourmet vegetarian restaurant. The group of speakers with whom I was going to dine was a very diverse and well-educated sampling of authors, archeologists, anthropologists, social and environmental activists, researchers, shamans, ceremonialists, and mystics, all from various parts of the world. They had most likely arrived earlier and would be expecting me. Not finding anything in the shop, I continued on my way toward the restaurant. Everyone else was already there, just seated, and my place at the table was waiting.

That night we enjoyed a sumptuous feast all together in a delightful garden courtyard under the stars. Each of the dishes consisted of vegetables and fruits, many of which are only found locally, prepared with holistic Mayan sensibilities. We were treated to wild mushrooms on buttery corn cakes, carrot and ginger soup, homemade corn tortillas stuffed with local cheeses, stewed squash flowers, a regional wild green called *chaya* which is very delicious and nutritious and is often prepared like steamed spinach, fresh vegetable salad with jicama root that tastes rather like water chestnut, juice of beet root mixed with fresh-squeezed orange juice, chilled coconut water, lush ripe papaya and mango, and on and on until we couldn't even look at another platter. We laughed, dined, drank, and conversed late into the wee hours. When the tropical birds in the patio began snoozing and the restaurant finally let us understand that they would be closing soon, I decided to head back.

It was a beautiful late night in the Yucatán and the nocturnal birds were calling from every tree in the plaza. The moon was shining brightly and the clouds were tinged with silvery pink from the moonlight. I had to pass by the same little shop again on my return walk. As I approached, I noticed that it was still open, which was very odd because it was extremely late and there were no customers inside. I heard the same strange voice calling to me once more as I neared the doorway.

"Psst. Now don't tell me you're going to pass me by?" it called out. "Really, aren't you going to get me out of here?"

Totally befuddled, I entered the shop again for one last look. "Excuse me for coming back so late, but I feel there's something in here that I need to search for," I tried to explain to the shopkeeper. "I have no idea what it is and this is a very peculiar feeling. Are you still doing business?"

"The hour doesn't matter," the owner said from behind a magazine. "It's all right. Come in."

The middle-aged shopkeeper assured me that I was welcome to look around all I liked. I inspected the shelves of first-quality reproductions and found nothing that could be calling out to me, nothing so completely unique. Then in a basket of stone carvings, while rummaging, I found one carving that looked different from all the others. It appeared to be older and more simple.

"Yea, it's me," I heard, as if the carving were speaking. "And it's about time!"

"What is this?" I asked the shopkeeper discreetly, as though I were just a tourist looking for gifts. Completely startled, I was feigning nonchalance.

The shop's owner wasn't fooled. "That's an ancient nature guardian," he said, "and if you are looking for that, you're being asked to protect something. That one you're holding is the only one like it here."

"I've never seen anything quite like this," I said. "What is it doing here?"

"Who knows?" the shopkeeper said and shrugged. "It just arrived by itself with the other things in that basket. You won't find many of those around anywhere, not anymore, not like that, not anything even close to it," he said. "That's one of a kind. It's old and we don't see many of those nowadays."

"Can I get this?" I asked. "Is that permissible?"

"Yes, you can," he said, putting the magazine away and scratching his tousled, wavy hair.

"This is what I've come for then," I replied. I felt I was on a rescue mission.

The shopkeeper nodded and lovingly wrapped the little guardian in a soft red cloth. I walked out with it, rather amazed. As I continued on, the experience became even more nonordinary. All the way back to the hotel I sensed that my bag was jumping and bouncing, singing and whistling, if one can imagine such an incongruous perception. I also felt quite unusual myself, and joyful, as if I were in an altered state. When I arrived in my room, I washed the little stone guardian and wrapped it back up again in its cloth. After I gently put this into my suitcase to pack for the return trip, the suitcase started the same shenanigans, humming and chattering all night. Somehow, I was supremely certain that my bag would not get lost in the air cargo area.

My flight left early the next morning so there was no time for anything else, no time to ask questions or investigate—otherwise I would have queried the local Maya about what I had rescued and what should be done, how this should be treated. The little guardian insisted on coming home with me and that was all. That was enough. There was no wait in customs, there were no obstacles of any nature, and I passed through like a gentle breeze. When I arrived at the airport of my hometown, my bag awaited me there at the baggage claim, seemingly buzzing and jumping imperceptibly, yet easily noticeable to my sensibilities of energy. It had miraculously arrived before I did! I had never encountered perceptions or occurrences even similar to this before. My new mission had been shipped to me, priority express.

I drove home with some trepidation and unpacked my bag immediately. I unwrapped the little guardian and while I did, it started to chirp. Setting it out in an area of honor on my altar to contemplate this, I gave it a seed offering, which is customary among the Maya as a token for nature spirits, and almost immediately I had to lie down on the love seat and Dream. I was heavy with trance. As I experienced the heightened awareness, I awakened directly into Dreaming and looked out of my living-room window. There is a tree that stands right outside it. The whole window was luminous and the glass had almost dissolved as if it were only a vapor. Underneath the tree stood a small dwarf dressed in an elegant suit, leading a tiny brown dog on a leash.

I was in utter shock. There are no dwarves that live in my neighborhood, not even in Dreaming, none that I know of, at least there had not been any! Jolted, I fell off the love seat and crawled to the window so as not to be observed by the dwarf. I stealthily peeped out with only my eyes above the level of the sill. He tapped his well-shod foot under the tree right outside my window as if he were waiting for someone. The little dog sat calmly and sweetly by his side.

I observed them both for quite some time. Suddenly, there was a flash of golden white light and I must have passed out or gone more deeply into the Dreaming. I was at a higher level of awareness, as though I had gone up on an elevator, opened the door, and found myself outside under the tree with the dwarf. There was no real linear transition. I had simply moved through a dissolving energetic barrier with my awareness and luminous body.

"Hello," the dwarf said. "I'm married now and my wife is from here. She's big. She doesn't like to walk this little dog, so I do it."

"Do you live in this neighborhood?" I asked in utter amazement.

"I do now," he replied. "I'm protecting this Tree of Life." The dwarf looked at me and smiled. "You can help me if you like. I'll help you, too. I'm here to take life part of the way home."

He was so endearing, I wanted to cry out and hug him. I felt such joy and tenderness. I didn't even have time to reply with "yes." Before I could, I was moved energetically yet again. I seemed to wake up at another level of perception. Now I was the only one who waited outside my window, under the beautiful tree, and I was in a paradise garden.

All at once, appearing in front of me, there was the most exquisite angel of light, more resplendent and radiant than I had ever imagined. I couldn't see anything but that light, and then after my eyes grew accustomed to it, I could just barely make out the silhouettes of the scenery on account of the splendor.

"Hello," the angel said. "What are you doing under my tree?"

I gasped. It was the winged shadow being I had seen under the tree at don Juan's, appearing in a different guise.

"Yes?" the angel said. "I thought it was about time to visit with you again."

"What are you doing in my front yard?" I asked like an idiot.

"Is that where we are?" he said. "I've come to show you something. I'm destroying this Tree of False Knowledge. It's time, and I've been called upon to do it. I want you to see it now. I won't harm you, though. I love you."

The tree split open with a shaft of lightning and the top burned to a singe. The two sides of the split trunk fell to the ground in flames. And it was the time for it. I watched in awe. As the tree burned, I was hoisted up on a celestial filament by a beautiful, luminous lady of cosmic golden light whose head was surrounded with a glowing disk, like a nimbus. She resided in a Pure Land of Light into which our human bodies may evolve, by becoming bodies of pure energy. I went up, up, up, inside a translucent shaft, and awakened there to still another level of aware-ness. I was seated under a tree rooted in a cloud, looking up at an eagle perched peacefully in the branches, seeing farther on into the shining golden blue sky beyond. I had been rising up a ladder of heaven.

I awakened back on my love seat. The experience was so present that it was impossible to move. I was overwhelmed by what I had seen. The Dreaming and visions had been so vivid, unquestionably real life, that they had lifted me into joy and toward an evolution beyond this life. They also foretold what was to come, though at that moment, I was totally unaware of this. As I roused myself, I found there was a message on my answering machine. It invited me to attend a local ceremony. The Tibetan monks from the Drepung Loseling Monastery were visiting in my own hometown, offering a sand mandala and making the ceremony at one of our most sacred springs, which is a source of inexhaustible water in the area.

The next day I went to the spring for the opening ceremony and attended the making of the sand mandala. I was deep in silence and in contemplation of my visions. During the week while the mandala was being created, I visited with the monks every day. I brought them sweets and returned to the site each afternoon until the mandala was finished and ready to be disas-sembled. At the closing ceremony, they offered the intent to the Cemetery Lords and to the Celestial Rainbow Being of transmu-tation, and to the Buddha of longevity, for the benefit of all sen-tient beings, asking that this energy stay a while longer and teach. There was great harmony with the wisdom of Mesoamerican shamanism.

Following the closing ceremony, I went with the monks in procession as they offered the rainbow-colored sands to our sacred spring. Upon concluding, one of the monks then turned to me and said, "Now we will go to New York."

Shortly after this, a portentous and foreseen climax came. The Twin Towers exploded into flames in New York City. Scenes of the fireball and the burning, falling towers were everywhere, in every media. It was exactly the vision I had been shown of the splitting tree: dividing, burning at the top, and then crashing to the ground. I realized that this experience had been foretold to me. I had been forewarned and given a message regarding what was happening and why. I was somewhat prepared for it because of the revelations, but I also saw that most of humanity had not been prepared. They were in shock, agony, denial, or delusion and could not understand. They were suffering.

There were altruistic guides among them, energetic and human, trying to protect life from impending, unnecessary war, devastation, and more suffering. Meanwhile a confused, angry, arrogant humanity was having another look at the destruction of Babel, this time man-made. The suspicion, accusations, and threats went back and forth. The anxiety and the level of suffering in human beings escalated.

I meditated upon this global tragedy for months following the event and asked for clarifications in my visions and in my Dreaming. How did we get to the place of such mutual misunderstanding? Why do we try to make life so "big," and at the same time so petty and so divisive? Isn't it possible to forgive and to have compassion for one another, alleviate suffering, and find true happiness and freedom with our brief time in human life? Isn't that where all our efforts should be focused? What about mutual respect? If we cannot help one another, can't we at least refrain from doing one another harm? Isn't it just as practical and beneficial to pursue simple spiritual and moral values, such as kindness, generosity, honesty, altruism, and affection, as it is to pursue economic ones? Are these all not of equal value and interdependent? Must we apply unwise force rather than reconcile? Is our capacity for lust, ignorance, anger, hatred, envy, religious dogma, knowledge, and power more important than our capacity for happiness and freedom? Can't we respect the right of each being to find happiness and make spiritual, moral, and economic choices, as long as this does not harm another being's ethical possibility or freedom to do so?

In all of my meditations and in the study of Dreaming, in the revelations following ceremonies, offerings of intent and prayers, and in contemplation, I kept arriving at the same conclusions. Ultimately, we ask for more happiness and freedom. As humans, even as animals, affection and compassion are necessary basics for survival and for that attainment of happiness and freedom. We must be able to progress then beyond animal and human to reach the evolutionary potentials that await us there. We need to work together, cooperatively. In that altruistic realization of joy, enlightenment, and unity, there is no conflict of duality, no war of opposites, genuinely.

Practice Eight

The Medicine of Realizing Emptiness

1. This Dreaming practice is in harmony with the Bon Dreaming practices of pre-Buddhist shamanism in Tibet. The intent is to realize the illusory nature of all form and thus experience the original deconfigured joy; the luminous nature of the sacred emptiness of being.

2. Enter into Dreaming each night with the intent to be awake and lucid within that state, to realize that one is Dreaming while one is actively engaged in it. This awareness is akin to the waking realization that all form is temporal illusion. Form is like a reflection in an empty mirror that dependently or artistically arises. It is actually the energy that makes the empty mirror and its reflections possible that is truly of interest, not the phantasmagoria.

3. Receive the messages from each Dreaming sequence with gratitude but stop there. Also, do not manipulate the Dreaming in any way or attempt to act in any manner within the scheme of Dreaming.

4. Instead, once the messages of an initiating Dream sequence have been received, before the Dreaming changes form, attempt to dissolve the entire scene into golden white light emptiness and maintain the awareness there.

5. A good mantra to use for this practice is the statement that the Buddha made upon reaching enlightenment sitting under the *Bodhi* tree: "Oh gods of my ego, you do not exist." Another excellent mantra is: "Form is empty. Empty is form."

6. Continue with this practice until you can dissolve any form, either in awakened Dreaming or in the waking Dreams of ordinary everyday life, into their deconfigured state of natural golden white empty luminosity.

7. There is no fear or control whatsoever within this state. It can be pure natural joy with the realization of nonattachment. There is a high level of awareness and bliss that frequently accompanies this realization, as it is an aspect of enlightenment.

8. The only thing that one is asked there is to consider making the decision to return to the world of form for the benefit of other sentient beings who are not yet liberated, perhaps to teach, so that others too might have a better chance of training their minds and attaining realization.

9

Practical Empowerments

Following the beginning of global crisis in 2001, it became evident that it was necessary to offer up energy in a powerful ceremony with an intent toward global healing and liberation. I contacted a friend of mine in Belize—a young Mayan priestess—and her apprentice niece and asked them if they would accompany me and offer in the ceremony. They agreed with the intent and the invitation was accepted. It would be the first time in more than five hundred years—since before the conquest—that a Mayan priestess had made the correct and traditional offerings openly in the sacred sites we selected, and it would be the first time this had ever been done in harmony with a culture outside the Mayan culture.

We would go to temple sites in the Yucatán honoring the sacred feminine, principally a sacred well and a temple site dedicated to priestess energy, Uxmal, and also to sites honoring the energy of the spiritual warrior, placing emphasis on the foremost site of realization in the Yucatán, Chichén Itzá. My friend is a direct descendant of one of the lineages of the Itzá, where the cultures of the Toltec and the Maya reached an apex and a sacred marriage, and so it would also be an offering to her Mayan ancestors. The secondary intent of the series of ceremonies was empowerment of the sacred feminine, which we felt was the key to the transformations we now seek in the world.

A ceremony of global healing and female empowerment was planned and we invited some of my students to join us. International women from all over the world were invited to attend, with more than sixteen cultures represented, novices in Dreaming, and even one of my editors in publishing. However, I was admonished by my Mayan friends and guides, priestesses and healer priests not to reveal everything that was occurring or was to take place to the women in attendance, for they were not letting go of all of their worldly ways yet. They were coming to the ceremony instead for a boost and for a little knowledge to aid them in living their lives.

We transcended more than five hundred years of conquest and made a piece of the original Mayan ceremony and multicultural collective sacred feminine offerings of rites of passage at two beautiful sacred caves, and at Uxmal and Chichen Itzá. Once it became appropriate and the energy had accepted our presences and intent there, we also began Dreaming with the novices. Through our guided collective offerings and our heart-filled intent we cleansed and elevated the woman's path of love from some of its misconceptions and energetic divisions, beginning with the myth of Eve and moving forward, clearing away the debris of former wrongs.

This was a highly practical undertaking. The ceremony offered is called a Primicia, which means "the first step," and it was truly a first step into a new era for women and for the sacred feminine, and thus also for men and for their relationships with women partners and colleagues, and with their feminine aspects. The offering reinitiated the contact between our worlds in the way it should have occurred more than five hundred years ago, with women at the forefront, in harmony, joy, and freedom, without slavery or exploitation.

The ceremony began the reinstatement of women's wisdom as a chalice and an equal and a necessary educational counterpart in relationship to the masculine energy. Many women at the ceremony were still in conflict. I realized at this gathering that most women still feel very wounded and as though they are under attack. They have lost contact with their purity and with their masculine aspect, their brother selves or their other halves, and with the men, with true lovers as men, with loving faithful husbands, fathers, functional sons, and so forth.

Yet the divisions and dysfunctions that have been created—the anger, the abuse, the abyss of misunderstandings, the fear, envy, and struggles—are meanwhile causing nations, houses, and relationships to crumble. The vicarious relationship we have with knowledge is not enough to allow us to reach one another and truly merge in loving union, which many long for. This forms a barrier to healing. Our quest for human perfection has turned us into a machine of ethnic and genetic cleansing, into a mechanism of sexual anger, and into a mere factory of human reproduction. So where are our true human values?

I saw more clearly than ever the wisdom of doña Celestina, for my house was rising out of its ashes, into life, in union, not split apart like the falling Tree of False Knowledge. I prayed in private over this each and every night. I saw that doña Celestina is correct, in that many women cannot seem to realize that there are too many people in the world already. Women are still trying to be mothers as an archetypal goal. Thus they are dissatisfied. They have not discovered the energetic healer priestess within themselves or the value of celibacy, or of celestial tantra, sacred sexuality.

Women have not made themselves ready for the initiations of highest tantra—energetic sexuality that leads to the realization of emptiness, to enlightenment, and to liberation. Many women of today still behave like butterflies who are born to be beautiful, reproduce, and then die after a brief life span. Some women of our day seek to be priestesses of illusion for the purpose of their satisfaction and strive to capture all of creation in the earthly healing solace of a mystical isle, which becomes just another shabby prison surrounded by shark-infested waters, once the intent not to let go is revealed. We need to move on and release; make a completely fresh start. Most women do not yet realize the wisdom, which comes from the longevity and continuity of enlightened awareness, rather than merely from the longevity of one lifetime, or from ancestral longevity.

This is certainly not only their fault. Our human nature is culpable, and so now is a good time for us to take the reins again. All aspects of wisdom need to work together now, for history has proven over and over again that Earthly ancestral lineage connections can be wiped out, damaged, or severed for a long time. Nothing is permanent, not even Mother Earth. Her myths and their remedies are transitory, and evolving being will eventually outgrow them.

Now is the time for pooling resources and for cleansing the ways between us with integrity. Now is the time for abandoning lesser divisive intents. Now is the moment to listen and to end these conflicts, to evolve and transcend boundaries and to begin anew with forgiveness and compassion. If we do not do this, humanity may not survive.

One afternoon during the journey of sacred feminine offerings, I told part of the story of my encounters with the nature guardian, which is called an *alux* in the Mayan language, to our group of novices. I could not tell them all, for I had been asked not to do so. I was asked not to explain the essential divisions that are causing life to fall. That night in the pristine Yucatán, as we all went to our Dreaming tasks, I had another Dream of the sacred Tree of Life. This time the tree was covered with fruits. They were all disembodied little ears and the tree was shivering, listening to my every prayer. All the little ears shook like the dried seed pods and cocoons that are attached to pieces of reed and used to make the special rattles and leggings worn by the traditional dancers of Mexico. These rattles called the energies of the ancestors and those energies who played a part in the Creation.

I heard then the voice of the little dwarf speaking to me from the rattling ears, which had become like whispering mouths, sighing and moaning in the wind with longing, vibrating on the branches of the tree like trembling leaves.

"Don't forget about the children," the voice said. "Carlo wouldn't want you to completely abandon the children."

I sat straight up in my bed with a shuddering thrill of the caress of love and anguish and I started to weep. Not only had that message brought me my longing for Carlo, even though we are at one with one another, but it had also brought me the illusion of the seeming impossibilities of this world, and it had addressed the most sensitive area in my life. Neither of us, not Carlo or I—in fact none of us, not even don Juan—had ever had any children really and truly of our own, because of very hard, harsh circumstances and childhoods, and new ideas. I couldn't go back to sleep and I stayed up praying all the rest of the night.

Don Juan had told me that when I leave my physical body and the syntax of this world that worships the vicarious machine of knowledge, and I occupy my energetic body fully, that then what I will long for will be an entirely different matter, realizable, an indivisible zero point, and that he will be united with me in that intent. Until such time it is like making love through open windows and we enjoy what we can have, always waiting for the moments when the mirror is empty and becomes a vessel that can transfer energies between the worlds.

It was logical for the energy to ask of me an offering of something, anything; consideration for the women who have had children and for the children themselves. After all, I was once a child trying to cross a solitary bridge, alone at night in a dark windy forest. I was a little girl listening to the night whisperings of an old woman in a dark basement. I was a nightingale singing in a tree at midnight. Carlo was once a little boy who didn't knock me from the branch of that tree with a slingshot. And don Juan was a luminous egg of light who shone down upon us both from the top sphere of that tree. All children should be so lucky.

Not all women and children have had the chance to understand love, or to behave as I have, nor have they had the opportunities that I have had. This was clearly and it was absolutely the most difficult thing that the energy could ever ask of me, especially after my harsh upbringing and my education with doña Celestina. I remembered then don Juan telling me that I am not responsible for all the death and the suffering in the world. "Just bring them your medicine," he said. "That's all you can do."

I saw them all hungry and wretched, huddling on the other side of a wall, abused, clamoring, and waiting for the medicine. The Dalai Lama of Tibet often says that even if we cannot help other sentient beings, at least we should do them no harm. I will advocate that much is certainly possible.

Carlo and don Juan are no longer in the world and this has definitely changed my heart. My heart looks toward the depths and the farthest points. It dwells in the most tender, inner, and infinite places that cannot be reached by the machine. I have compassion. With regard to helping others, people have actually come to me to beg for this. Don Juan recommended speaking in parables in such cases, and teaching when appropriate, little by little. Carlo recommended writing, and then there is direct transmission.

There are those innocents out there who haven't had a good chance yet. I accepted the tasks, and upon returning from the ceremony I began the energetic endeavor of writing this, my third book, to honor the three levels of the Tree of Life. It has been a pleasure, and it is necessary in order to bring all three levels to beings in this way.

I discovered in recounting that as a result of the tasks and the energetic empowerments, all of my labels were falling away. I had formerly been so pleased with my hard-earned titles of balam, nagual, shaman, and Dreamer. I had worked so hard for my education, for only the best, magna cum laude, high graduate status, and to earn my master's degree. I had faced life-threatening challenges and won, and transcended the human illusions of both immortality and the fear of death.

Now, all of that meant nothing, and when compared with the value of simple, genuine realization and affection, it was less than zero. Those titles were only words, glosses, compartments, beautiful suits of clothes that one may wear—but in the end they are not the whole of the heavenly wardrobe and are, in fact, limiting. I had transcended far more than the mere words. I had gone beyond the competitive ego syntax that wants more than the realization of emptiness. On my journey, I had seen through the delusions of illness and death. I had witnessed the resurrection itself before my eyes, perhaps for my eyes only, and had sojourned into the love and illumination that can survive death.

Still, I was a solitary warrior and traveler into the unknown, guided only by those who had gone before me and by the energy of the infinite itself. So I dedicate this final chapter to the women and men and children everywhere who are still struggling to acquire, to maintain, and to protect what they have, and who wish for what I have. The world of illusion is a challenge that leads us eventually to enlightenment. That is some comfort.

The Tibetans are correct that the best thing sentient beings can offer to the world is a chance to leave the carnival of delusion while still alive, or even at death if they sincerely ask for it. Thus to complete my task, in the writing of this book, I strove to offer a glimpse of what lies beyond the dance of the seven veils. I have a ticket.

I wish all of you love and peace, joy, freedom, and eventual illumination.

Practice Nine

Transforming the Dream of the Planet

1. This is currently my favorite practice, in harmony with the task that I have been given. To accomplish this, one needs to be able to send one's energy body beyond the confines of the solar system. Most of you will not be able to go that far without assistance, so first I will describe how I do this practice and then I will suggest a variation that will be accessible to everyone.

2. In Dreaming I ascend to a star. I will not locate the position on a star chart for you. It is a transcendent location. From that star, with my energy body blazing, I open one single eye at the core of my very being. From there, I gaze down upon the Earth and See what is needed.

3. I bathe the Dream of the planet and every malicious, fractious intent by sending love in the form of light and its life-giving nourishment, infinite generosity, the calm of peace, the illumination of understanding, and the vibrancy of joy.

4. This practice requires the loss of the human form, so that one does not Dream of oneself as a human body or as part of a human body. It is the loss of the human form that allows one to journey beyond the Earth and shapeshift into whatever nonhuman form is required. Thus the loss of the human form is like a thunderstruck death, and so do not be too eager to pursue it.

5. The novice Dreamer might instead intend to Dream of one's body as gazing down upon the celestial blue Earth from a

silvery space station. There is a clear window within the space station, aloft in the cosmos, which allows you to see the entire planet. You are protected and you smile.

6. From that vantage point, you may send down all your cleansed blessings upon the Earth and Dream them to be received by all of its inhabitants; all its sentient beings, microorganisms, insects, aquatic life, plants, wingeds, reptiles, animals, humans, all the elements, the living, the dead, and even inorganic awareness. Send happiness to all our relations, if you have ever experienced it, hope for freedom accepted with wisdom and love for the Mother Earth and her innate ability to achieve balance and harmony.

Epilogue

Thirteen Steps to
a Better Life and Death

From a very practical standpoint, all of these insights and experiences can be distilled into thirteen steps along the path to freedom and joy.

1. Listen. The first step would be to trust the truth of your own inner language at least as much as you trust the syntax of any limited cognitive system. In such a manner you become multilingual. Strive to corroborate the accuracy of your inner hearing, and foster sobriety, so as to increase it. Honor your own inner language and your inner hearing. Practice continually. Test the truths you receive by contemplating their guidance with fidelity and compassion. Then, as with anything, continually reprise, distill, and refine your understanding.
2. Heart. A good rule to remember in life is that the body doesn't lie, and the best guide in the body is an open loving heart. Follow your heart.
3. See. See all experience as a Dream. Original awareness is like a luminous empty mirror. That empty mirror is very clarified and malleable at its best, so that it functions rather like a window, or like a sheet of pure water, or as a two-way

mirror, rather than like a barrier of self-reflection, or a smoking obsidian, or a television screen.

4. Dream. Engage in wholesome practices such as Dreaming that awaken and nurture the developing energy body and the subtle mind, which are your vessel of evolution, your guide toward all healing, and the portion of your being that will journey into and beyond death.

5. Love. All being is sacred and needs to be treated in a sacred manner. Beginning or redirecting your life in this way will gradually release you from the fetters that are caused by the profane and abusive acts at other levels of awareness.

6. Tantra. Sexuality is very sacred and treating it in such a manner can actually transport human awareness toward the new archetypal relationships for which we so desperately long.

7. Respect. If you cannot behave in a beneficial manner toward another being, or regarding a situation, or toward a place, or toward even yourself, at least intend to and learn to do no harm.

8. Reciprocity. Practice reciprocity and honor the three levels of the Tree of Life, first the Underworld of Death, of the Ancestors, and of Primordial Sexuality; second the Creative Vital Realm of Mother Earth; and third the Celestial Realm of Cosmic Spirit and Subtle Mind.

9. Forgive. Forgive one another and respect the rights of all beings to attain happiness and freedom. Practice courageous, even unconventional wisdom, altruistic kindness, strong nonviolent compassion, humility, radical honesty, modesty, and generosity.

10. Offer. Make of yourself a living offering. See every opportunity and every experience as a step on the path of transmutation, refinement, and release.

11. Nonattachment. Hold on to nothing and do not make too

much of anything. Remember the inherent suffering of life at this level. At best this life is a mixture of pleasure and pain. Be mindful of this wisdom. Allow your love to grow bigger than any container that would eventually stifle it. Your heart can become as ample and as open as the sky.

12. Education. Always respect the process of education and seek to learn as much as it is possible to learn in this life, welcoming each moment and focusing on quality balanced with variety, rather than on mere quantity.

13. Courage. Never allow fear, habit, knowledge, or self-doubt to become insurmountable obstacles on your path. Anything is possible, one way or another. Being is so infinite and so unfathomable that if a thing has merit, it will find a proper way.

About the Author

Merilyn Tunneshende (pronounced Tune-shond), M.Ed., is the author of three books on shamanism, sacred evolutionary sexuality, enlightenment, and healing who concentrates on the development of the energy body as a vehicle for realization and liberation. Her most recent work focuses on beyond-death states. She has been involved with shamanism since childhood and formally so since the 1970s, and has academic degrees in Language Arts, Comparative Religion-Philosophy, and Education.

Books of Related Interest

DON JUAN AND THE POWER OF MEDICINE DREAMING
A Nagual Woman's Journey of Healing
by Merilyn Tunneshende

DON JUAN AND THE ART OF SEXUAL ENERGY
The Rainbow Serpent of the Toltecs
by Merilyn Tunneshende

THE TOLTEC PATH OF RECAPITULATION
Healing Your Past to Free Your Soul
by Victor Sanchez

DANCE OF THE FOUR WINDS
Secrets of the Inca Medicine Wheel
by Alberto Villoldo and Erik Jendresen

PSYCHONAVIGATION
Techniques for Travel Beyond Time
by John Perkins

SPIRIT OF THE SHUAR
Wisdom from the Last Unconquered People of the Amazon
by John Perkins and Mariano Shakaim Shakai Ijisam Chumpi

SHAMANIC EXPERIENCE
A Practical Guide to Psychic Powers
by Kenneth Meadows

VODOU SHAMAN
The Haitian Way of Healing and Power
by Ross Heaven

Inner Traditions • Bear & Company
P.O. Box 388
Rochester, VT 05767
1-800-246-8648
www.InnerTraditions.com
Or contact your local bookseller